GREAT SONGS FOR GUITAR

CHORD SONGBOOK
THE WHITE BOOK

All I Have To Do Is Dream • The Everly Brothers 3
Bring Me Sunshine • Morecambe & Wise 6
Crazy • Willie Nelson 8
Every Breath You Take • The Police 10
Golden Touch • Razorlight 12
Hallelujah • Leonard Cohen 16
Highway To Hell • AC/DC 18
How Deep Is Your Love • The Bee Gees 22
I Predict A Riot • Kaiser Chiefs 24
I Shot The Sheriff • Bob Marley 28
I Will Survive • Gloria Gaynor 30
Is You Is Or Is You Ain't My Baby? • Fats Waller 32
Run • Snow Patrol 34
Should I Stay Or Should I Go • The Clash 37
Viva La Vida • Coldplay 44
Wonderwall • Oasis 40
You Raise Me Up • Josh Groban 47

WISE PUBLICATIONS
part of The Music Sales Group
London/New York/Paris/Sydney/Copenhagen/Berlin/Madrid/Hong Kong/Tokyo

Published by
Wise Publications
14-15 Berners Street, London W1T 3LJ, UK.

Exclusive Distributors:

Music Sales Limited
Distribution Centre, Newmarket Road,
Bury St Edmunds, Suffolk IP33 3YB, UK.

Music Sales Pty Limited
20 Resolution Drive, Caringbah,
NSW 2229, Australia.

Order No. AM1004091
ISBN: 978-1-78038-374-3
This book © Copyright 2011 Wise Publications,
a division of Music Sales Limited.

Unauthorised reproduction of any part of
this publication by any means including
photocopying is an infringement of copyright.

Edited by Adrian Hopkins.
Produced by shedwork.com

Printed in the EU.

Your Guarantee of Quality:

As publishers, we strive to produce every book
to the highest commercial standards.

This book has been carefully designed
to minimise awkward page turns and to
make playing from it a real pleasure.

Particular care has been given to specifying
acid-free, neutral-sized paper made from pulps which
have not been elemental chlorine bleached.
This pulp is from farmed sustainable forests and
was produced with special regard for the environment.

Throughout, the printing and binding have
been planned to ensure a sturdy, attractive publication
which should give years of enjoyment.

If your copy fails to meet our high standards,
please inform us and we will gladly replace it.

www.musicsales.com

All I Have To Do Is Dream

Words & Music by Boudleaux Bryant

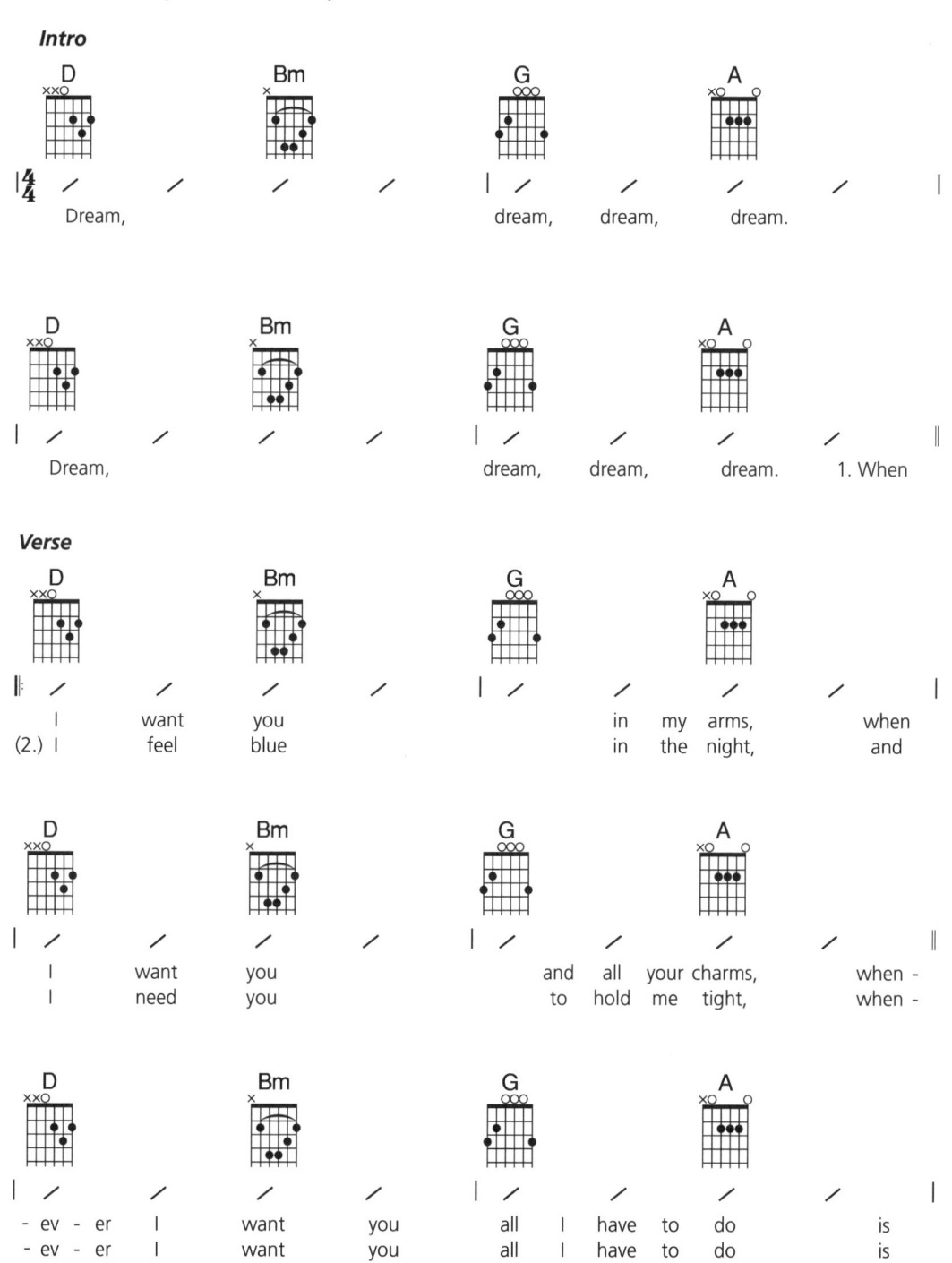

© Copyright 1958 Sony/ATV Music Publishing.
All Rights Reserved. International Copyright Secured.

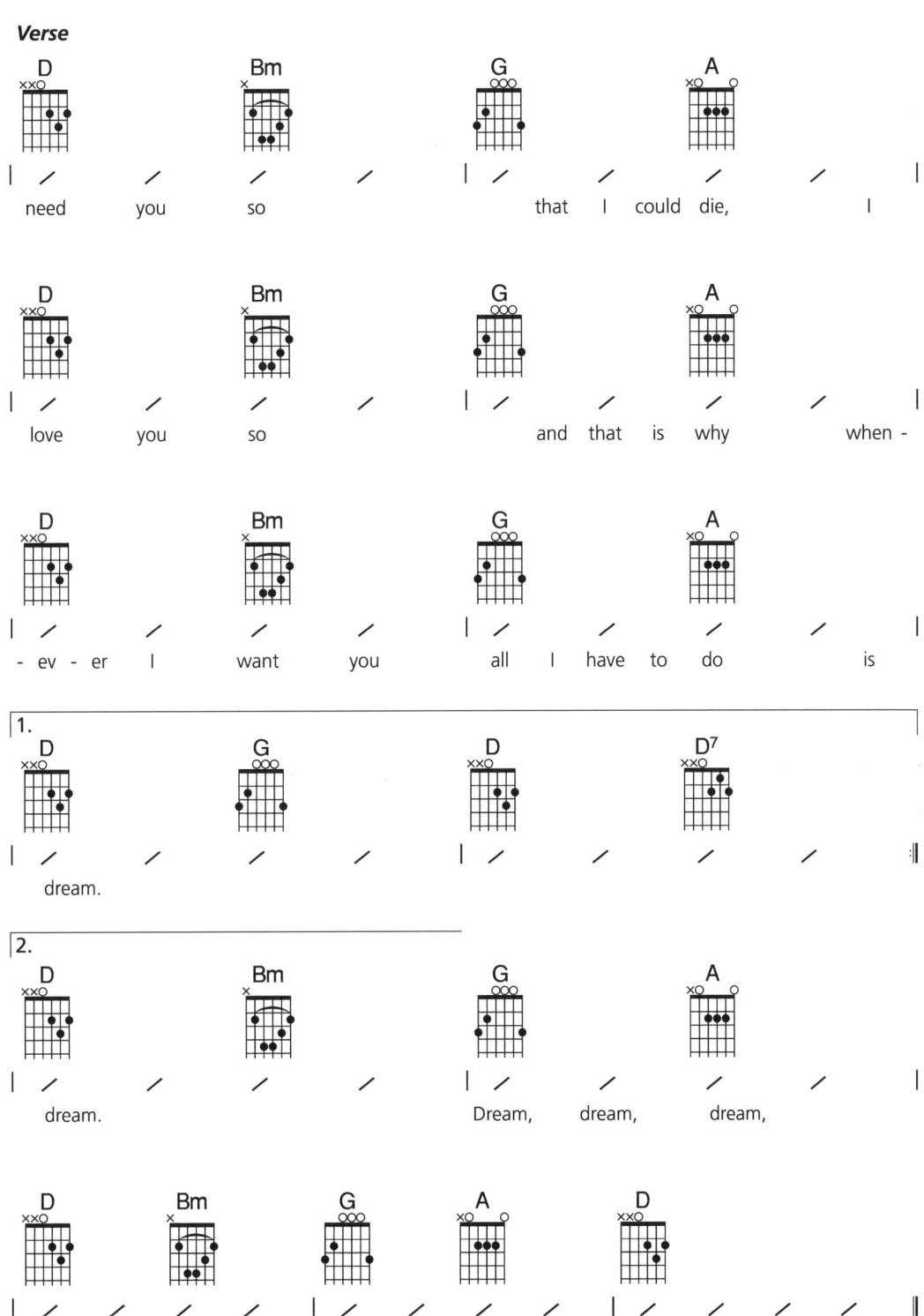

Bring Me Sunshine

Words by Sylvia Dee
Music by Arthur Kent

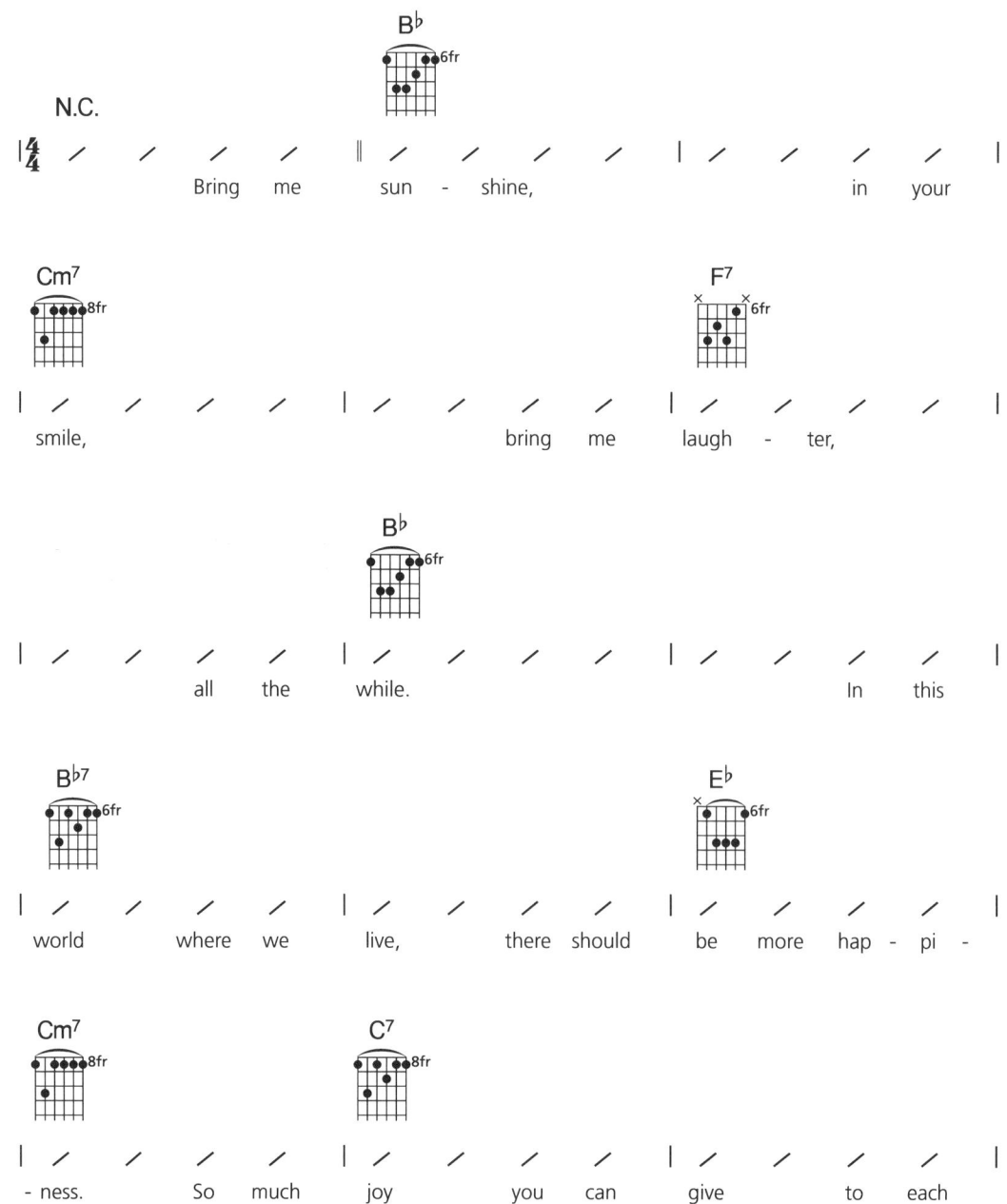

© Copyright 1966 (Renewed) Edward Proffitt Music/Music Sales Corporation (ASCAP) (50%)/
Arthur Kent Music Company/The International Music Network Limited (50%).
All Rights Reserved. International Copyright Secured.

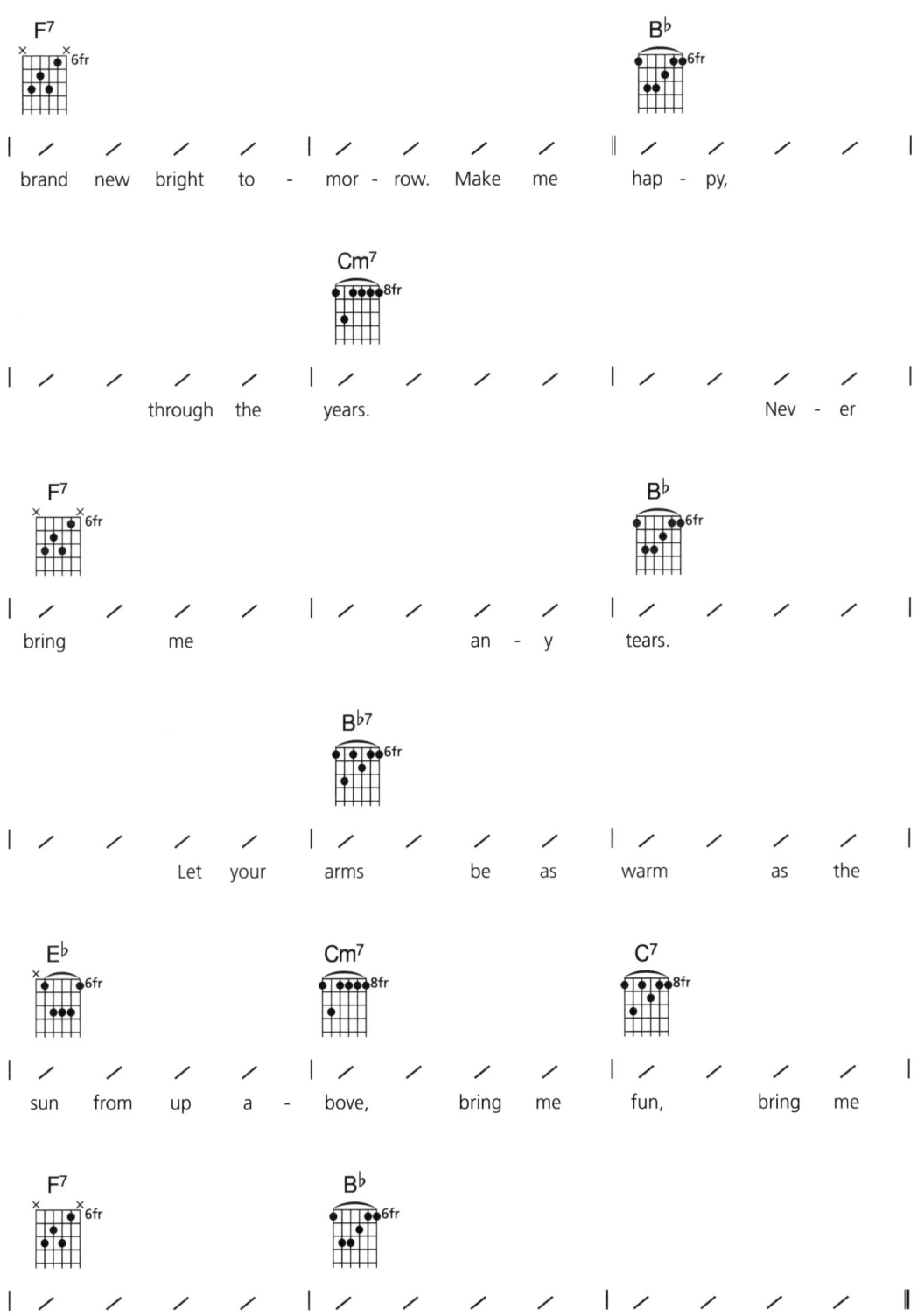

Crazy

Words & Music by Willie Nelson

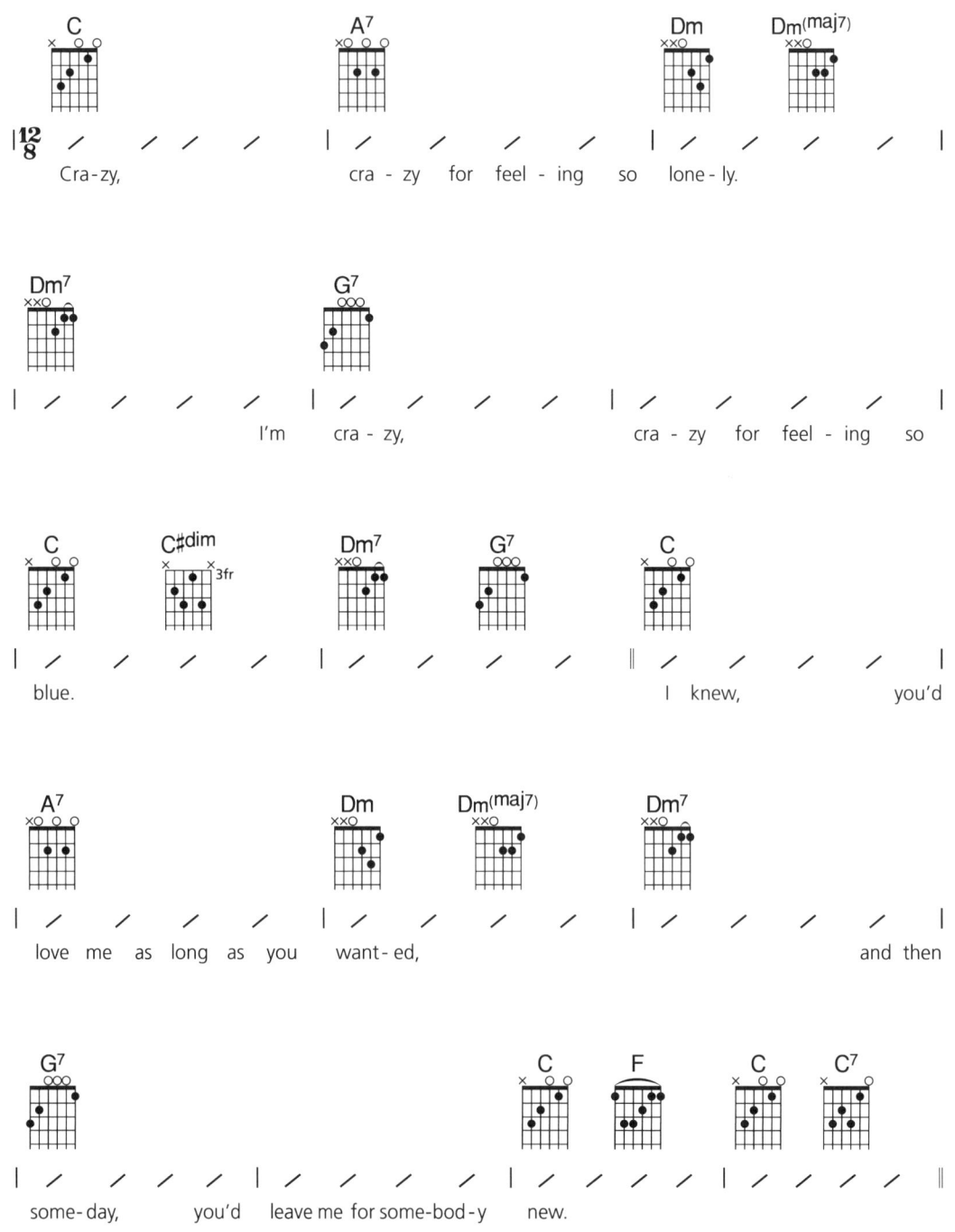

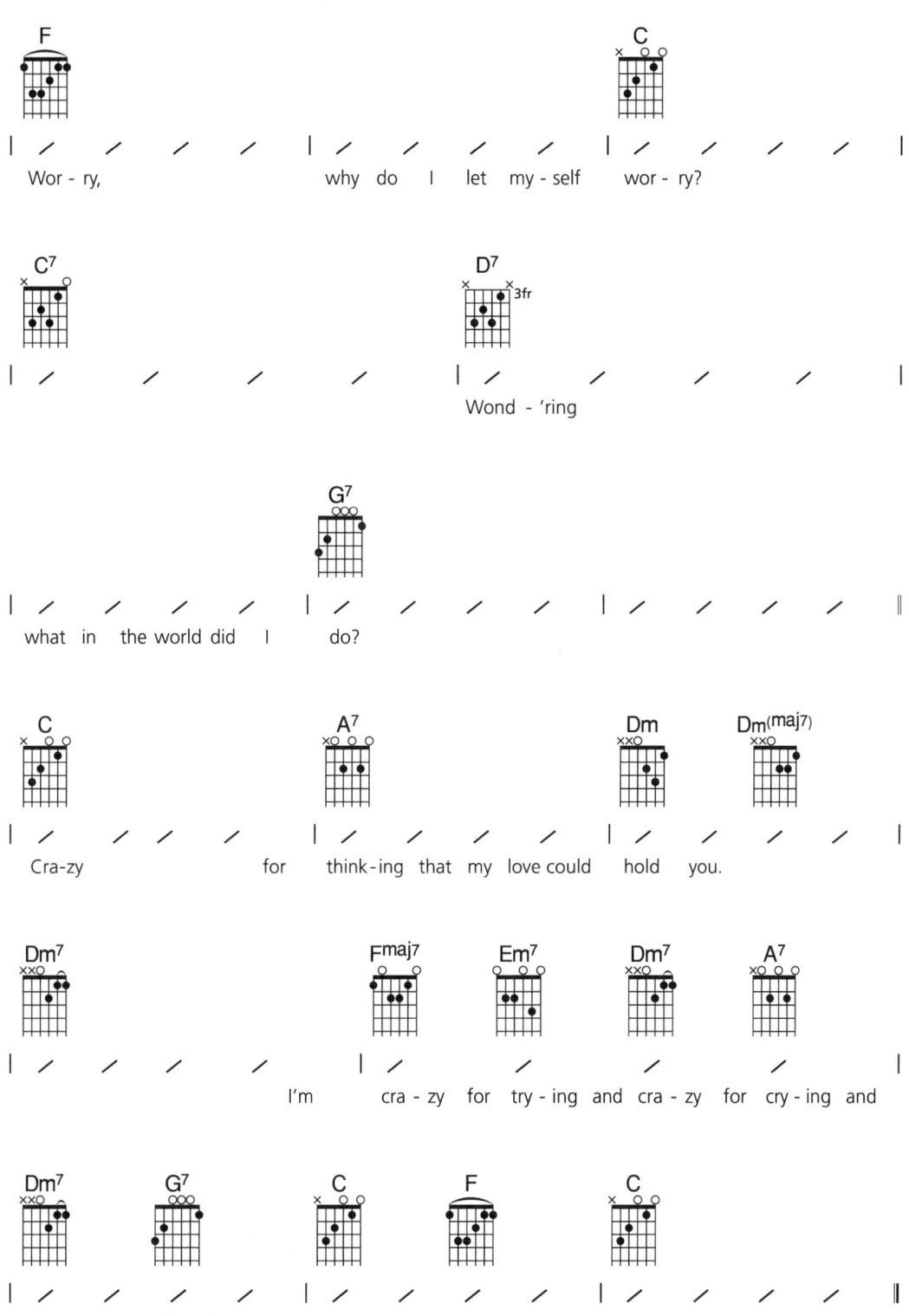

Every Breath You Take

Words & Music by Sting

4/4 N.C.

‖: **Aadd9** | | **F#m(add9)** |
1. Ev-'ry breath you take, ev-'ry move you make,

| **Dsus2** | **Esus2** | **F#m(add9)** |
ev-'ry bond you break, ev-'ry step you take, I'll be watching you.

| **Esus2** **Aadd9** ‖ | | **F#m(add9)** |
2. Ev-'ry sin-gle day, ev-'ry word you say,

| **Dsus2** | **Esus2** | **Aadd9** |
ev-'ry game you play, ev-'ry night you stay, I'll be watching you.

𝄋 | **Dsus2** ‖ **Csus2** | **Aadd9** |
Oh, can't you see you be-long to me.

| **Badd9** | | **Esus2** |
How my poor heart aches with ev-'ry step you take.

© Copyright 1983 Steerpike Limited/Steerpike (Overseas) Limited/EMI Music Publishing Limited.
All Rights Reserved. International Copyright Secured.

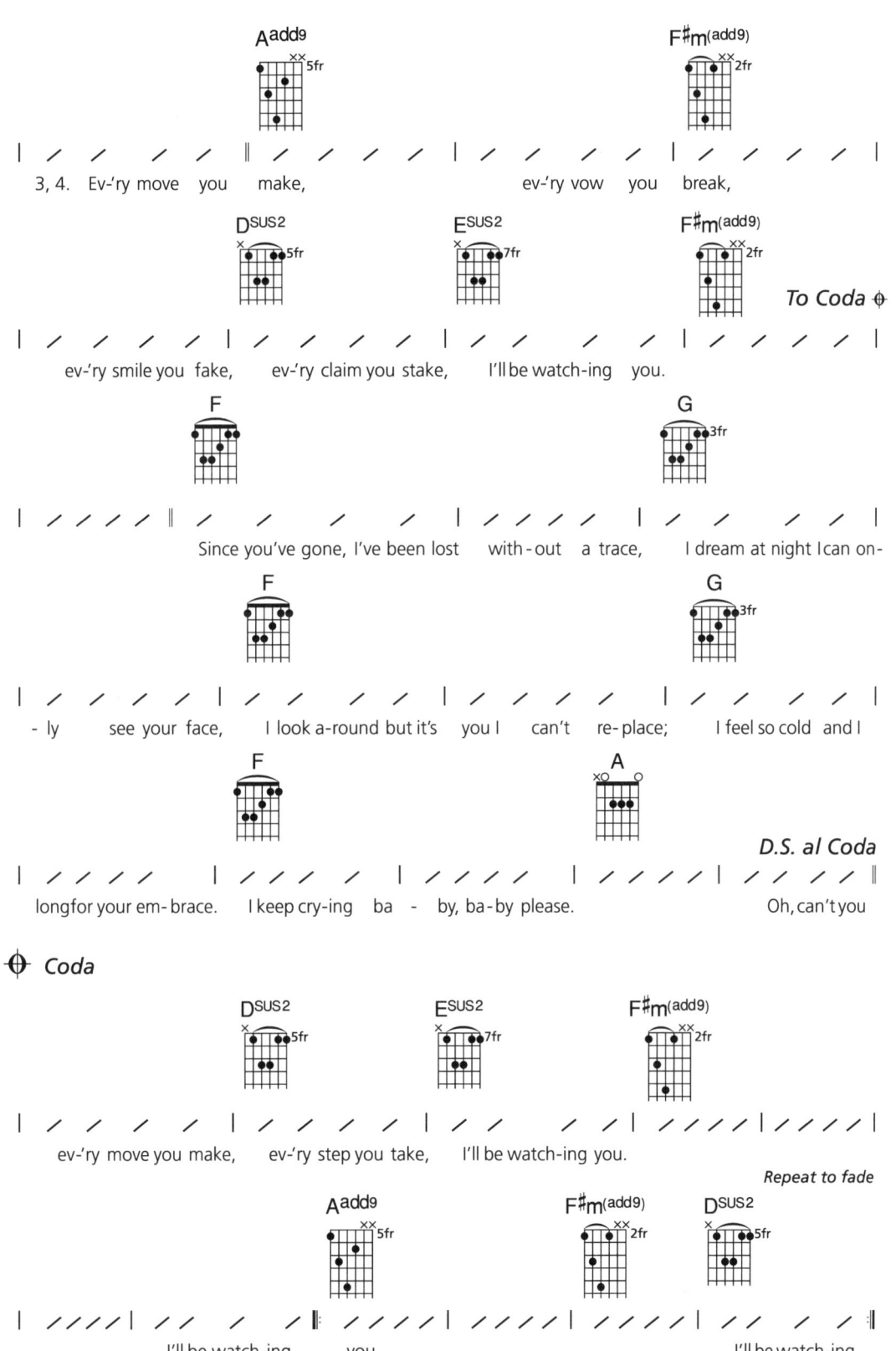

Golden Touch

Words & Music by Johnny Borrell

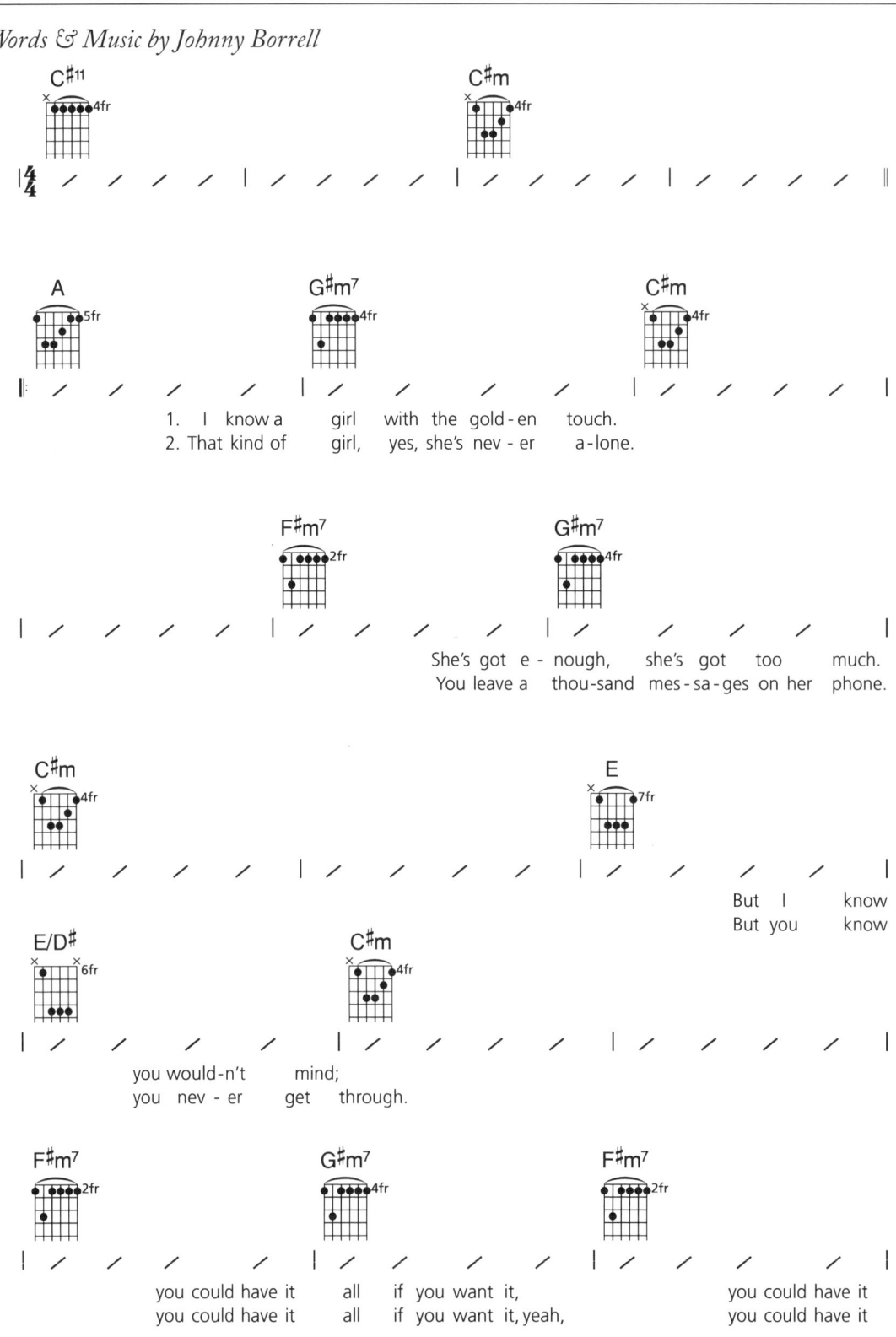

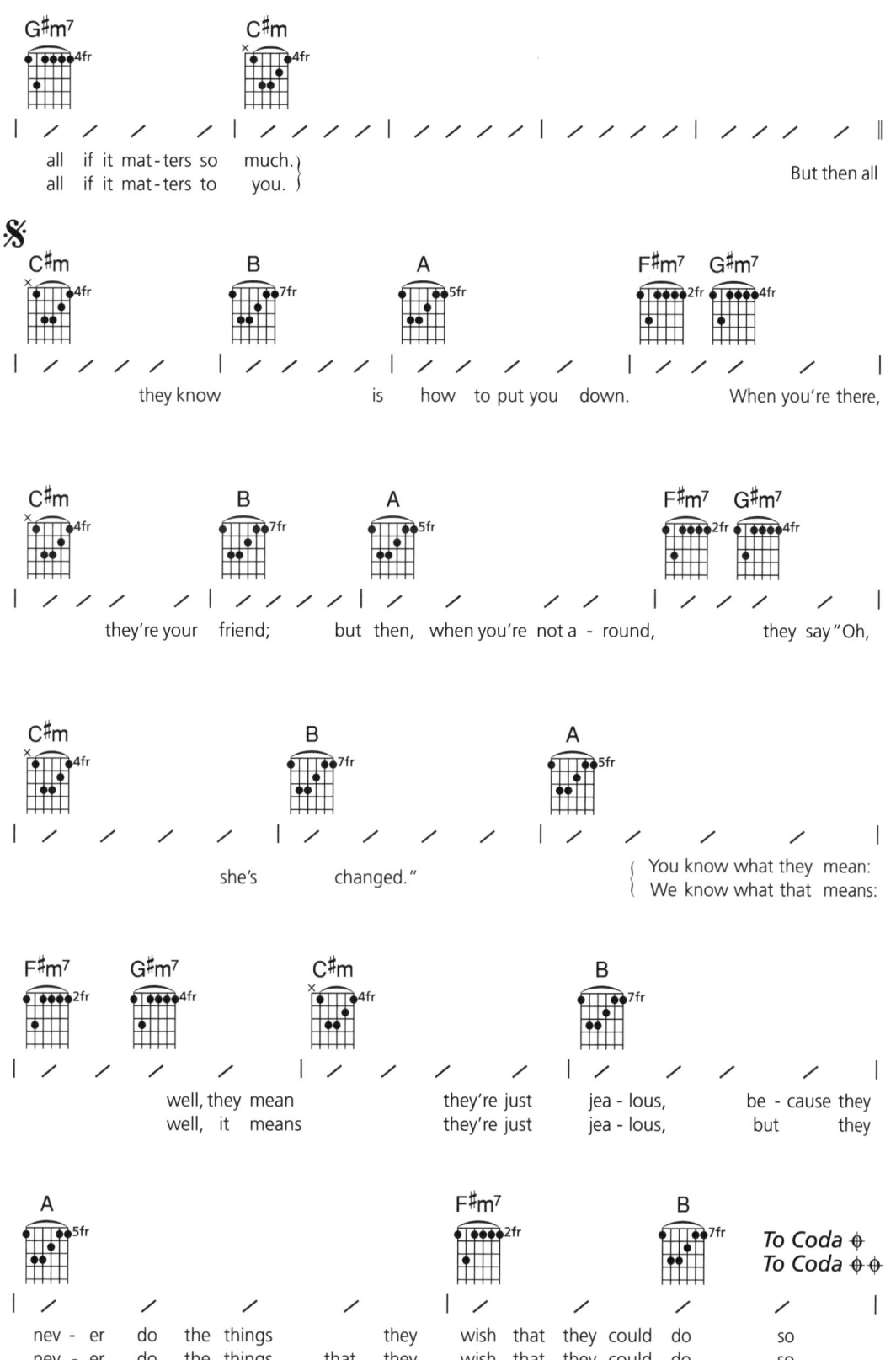

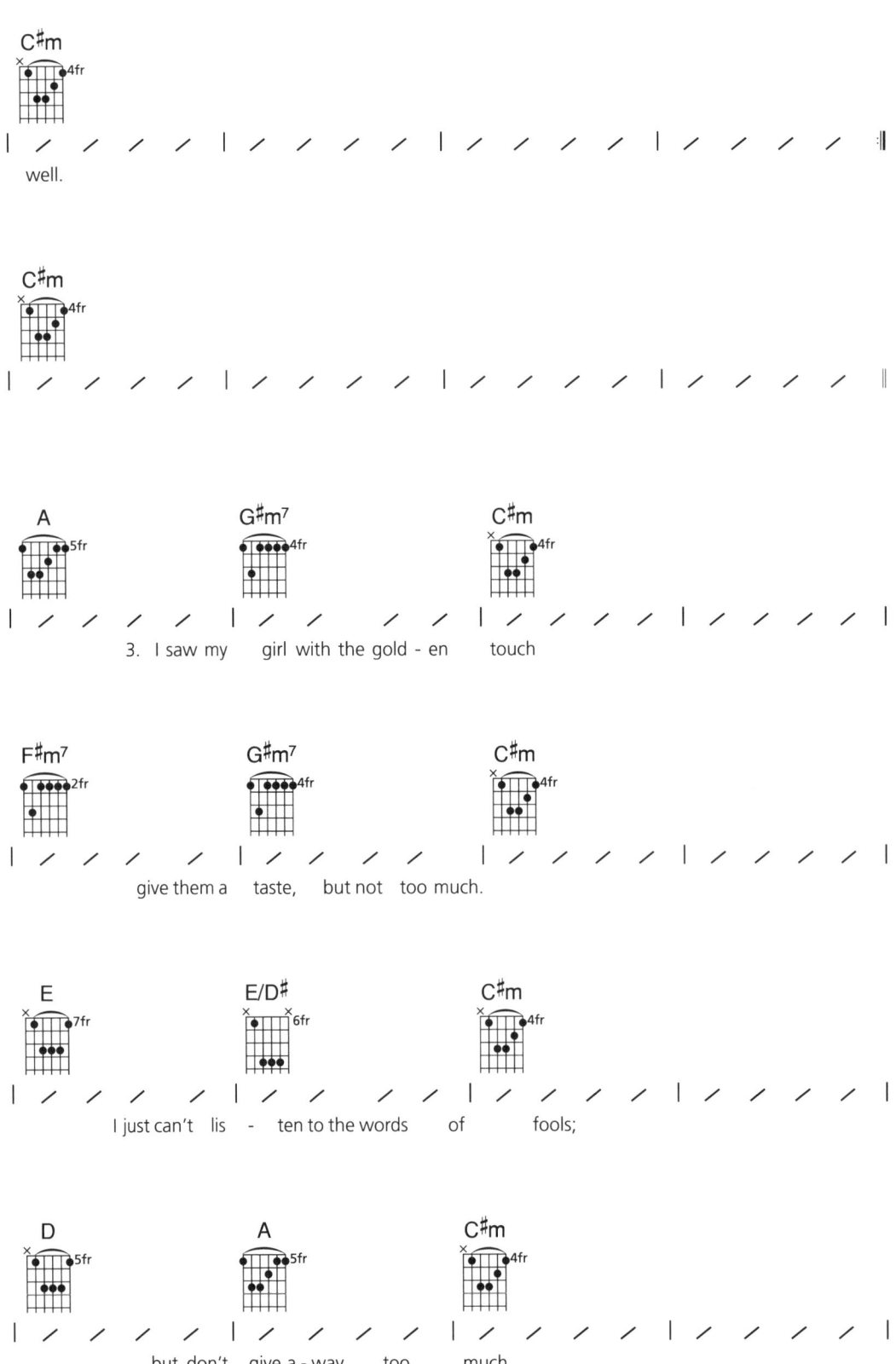

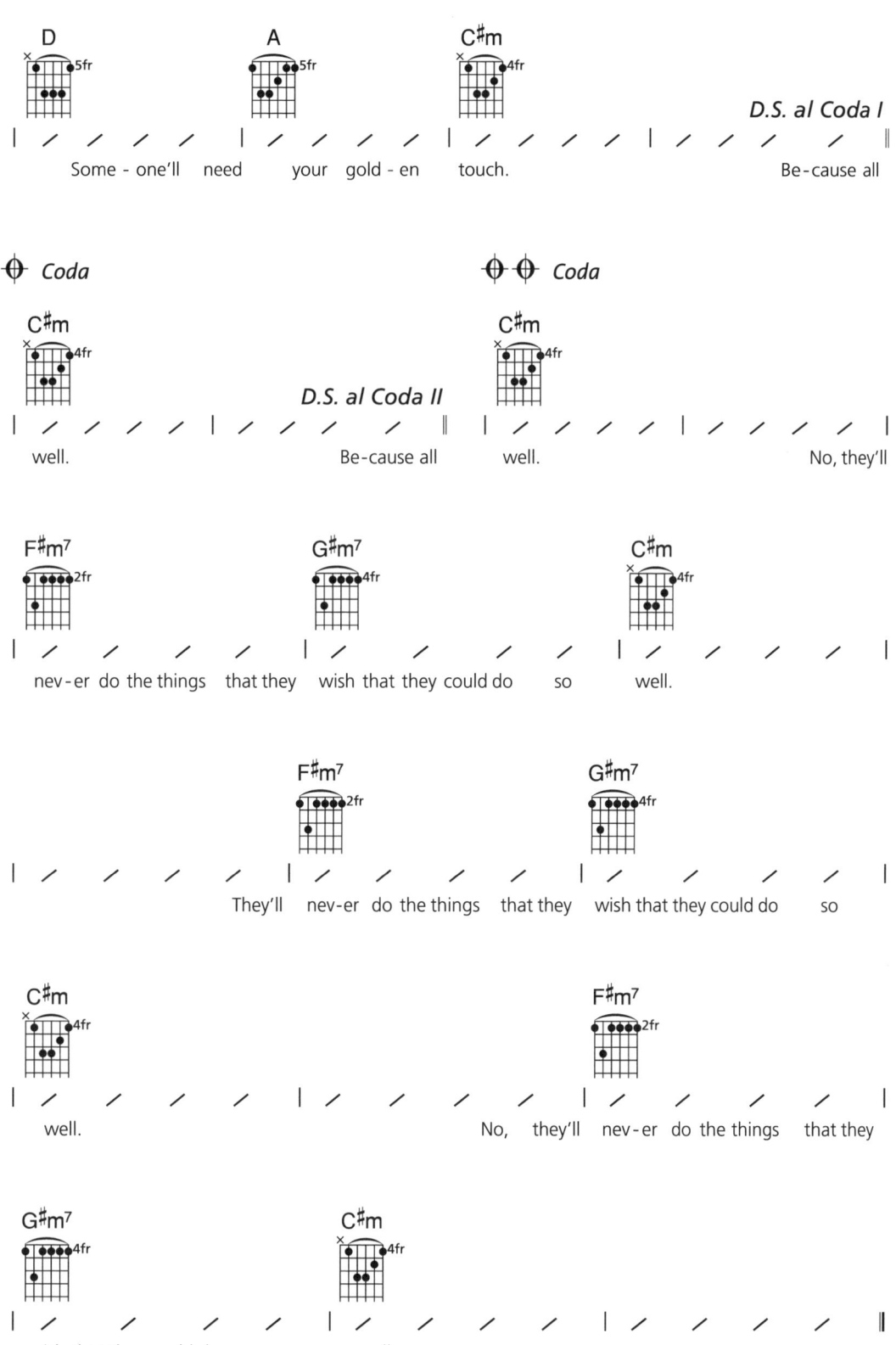

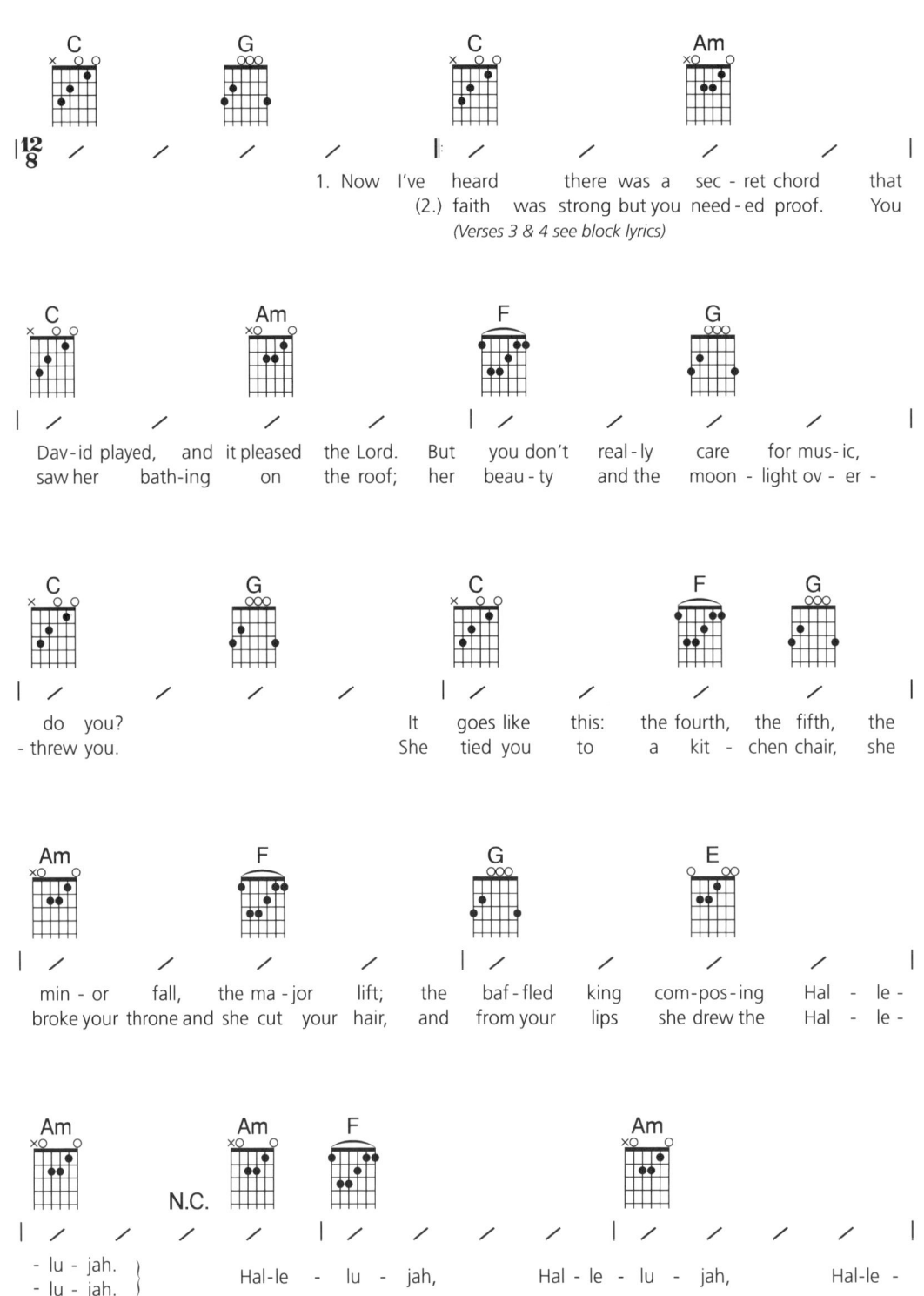

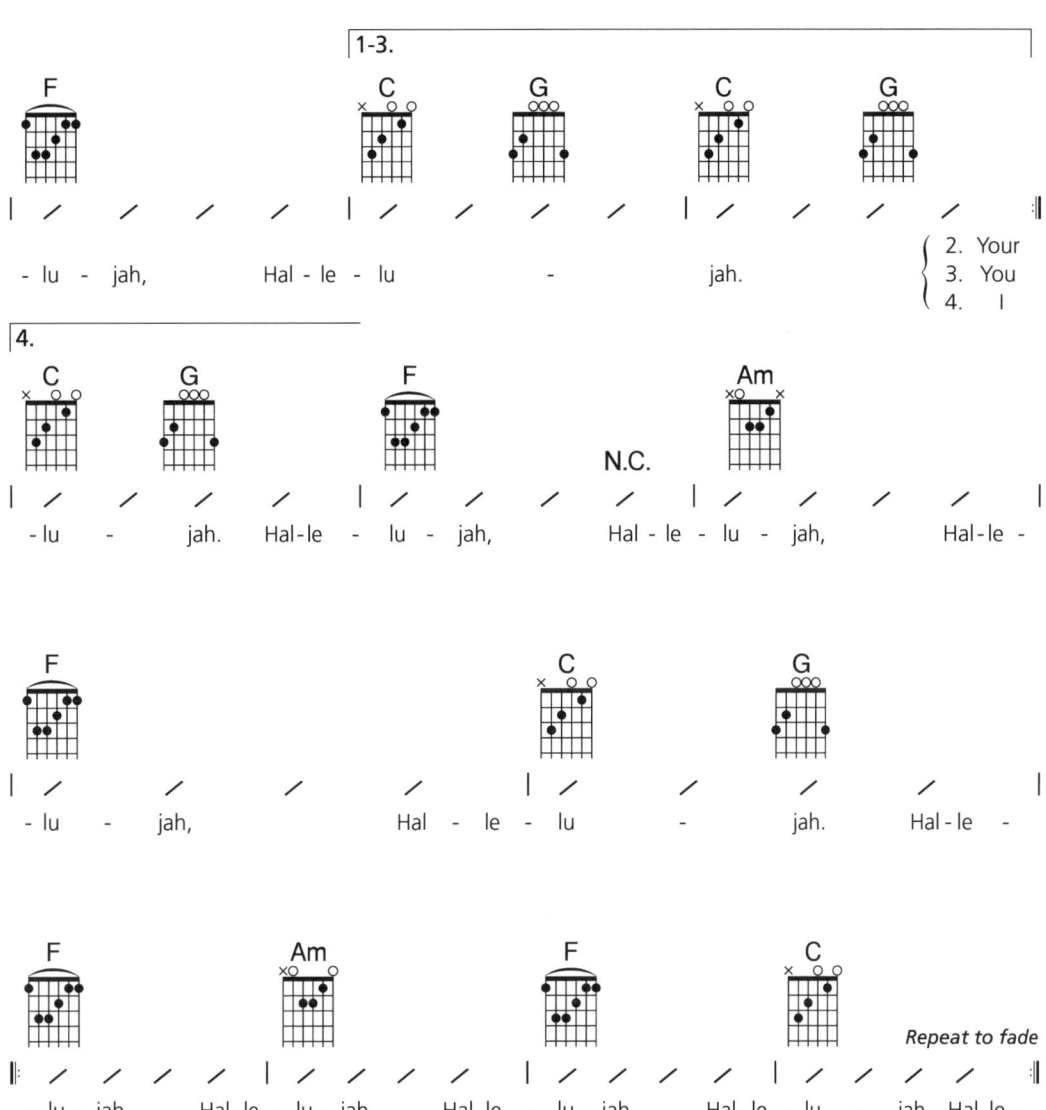

Verse 3
You say I took the name in vain
I don't even know the name
But if I did, well really, what's it to you?
There's a blaze of light in every word
It doesn't matter which you heard
The holy or the broken Hallelujah.

Hallelujah *etc.*

Verse 4
I did my best, it wasn't much
I couldn't feel, so I tried to touch
I've told the truth, I didn't come to fool you.
And even though it all went wrong
I'll stand before the Lord of Song
With nothing on my tongue but Hallelujah.

Hallelujah *etc.*

Highway To Hell

Words & Music by Angus Young, Malcolm Young & Bon Scott

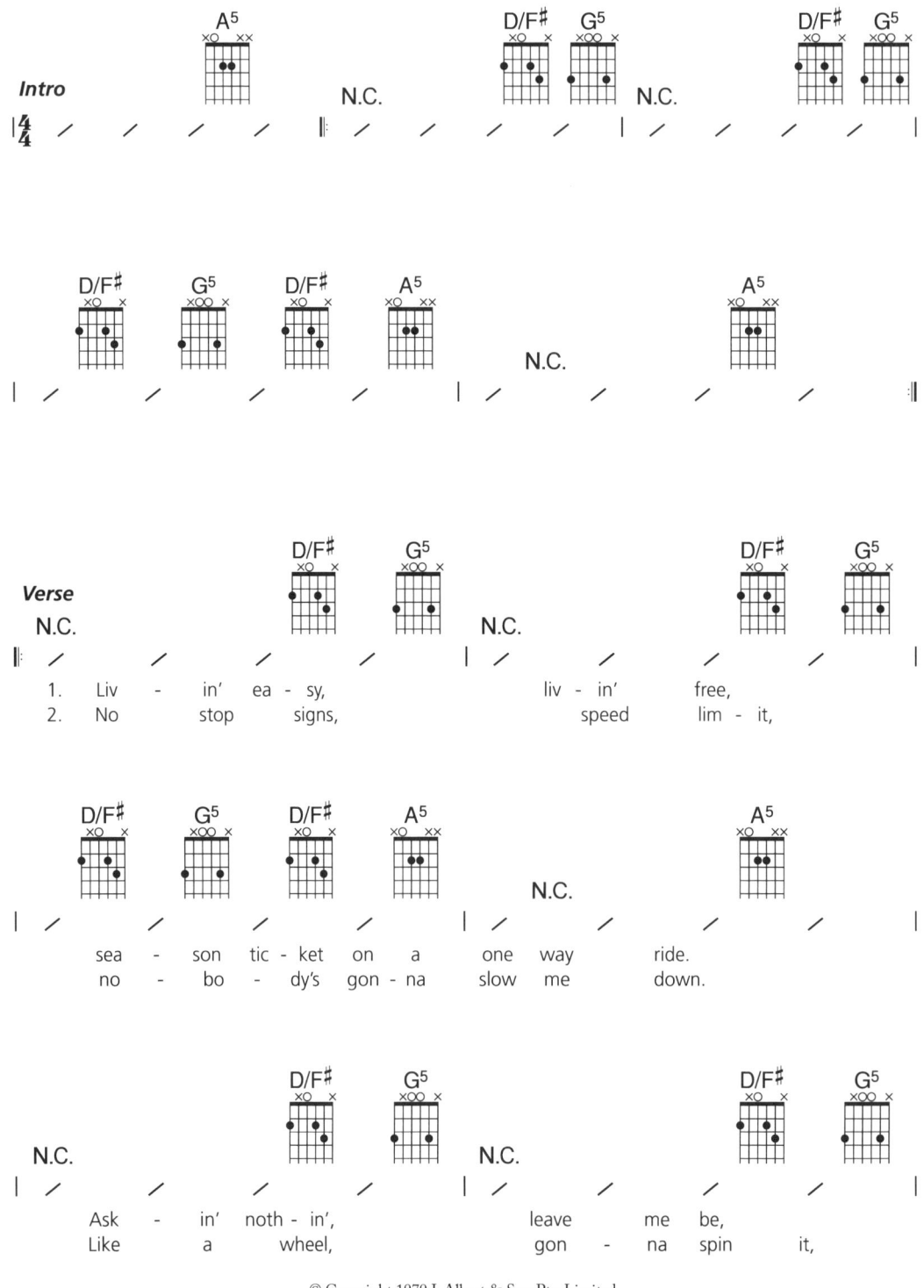

© Copyright 1979 J. Albert & Son Pty. Limited.
All Rights Reserved. International Copyright Secured.

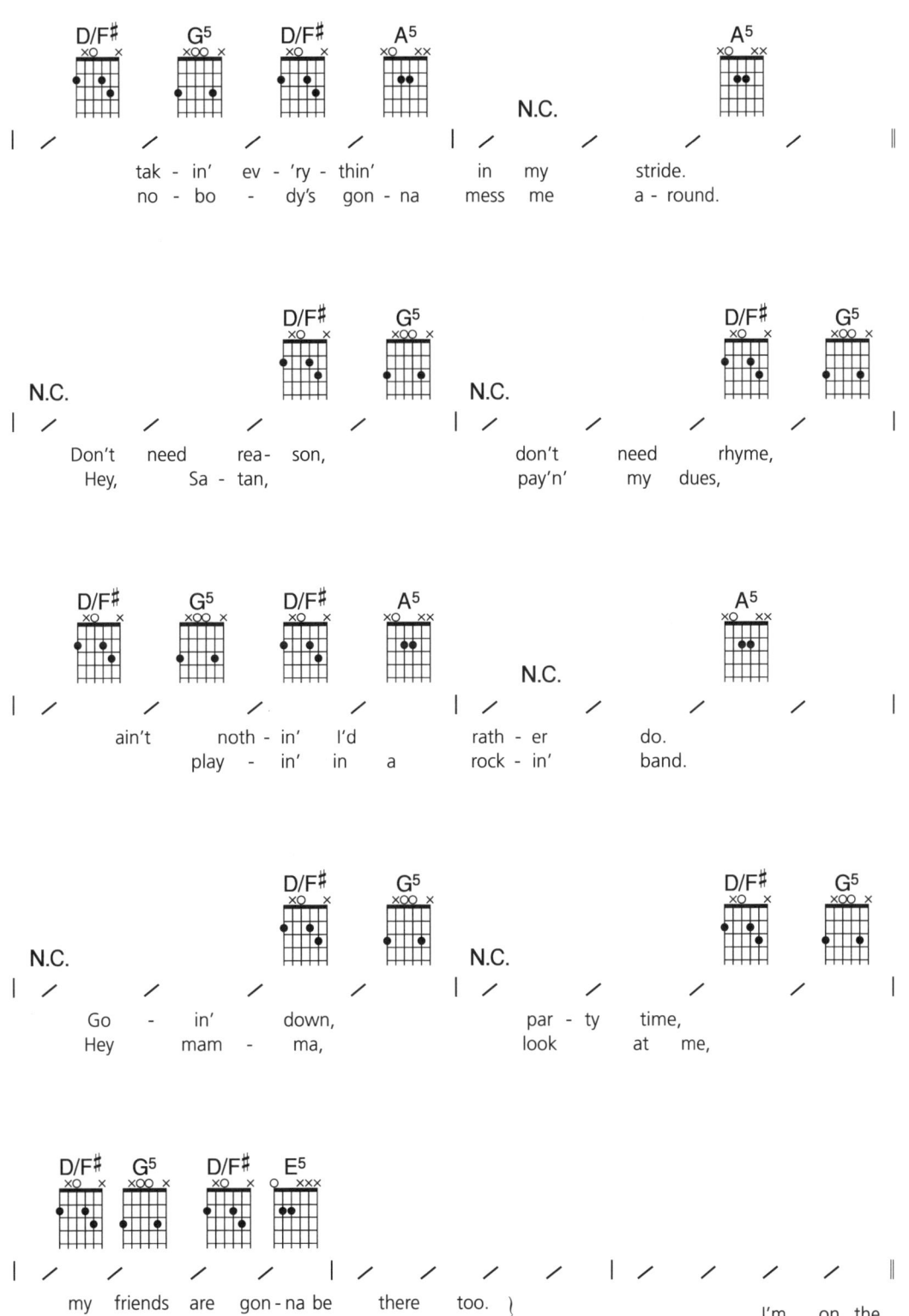

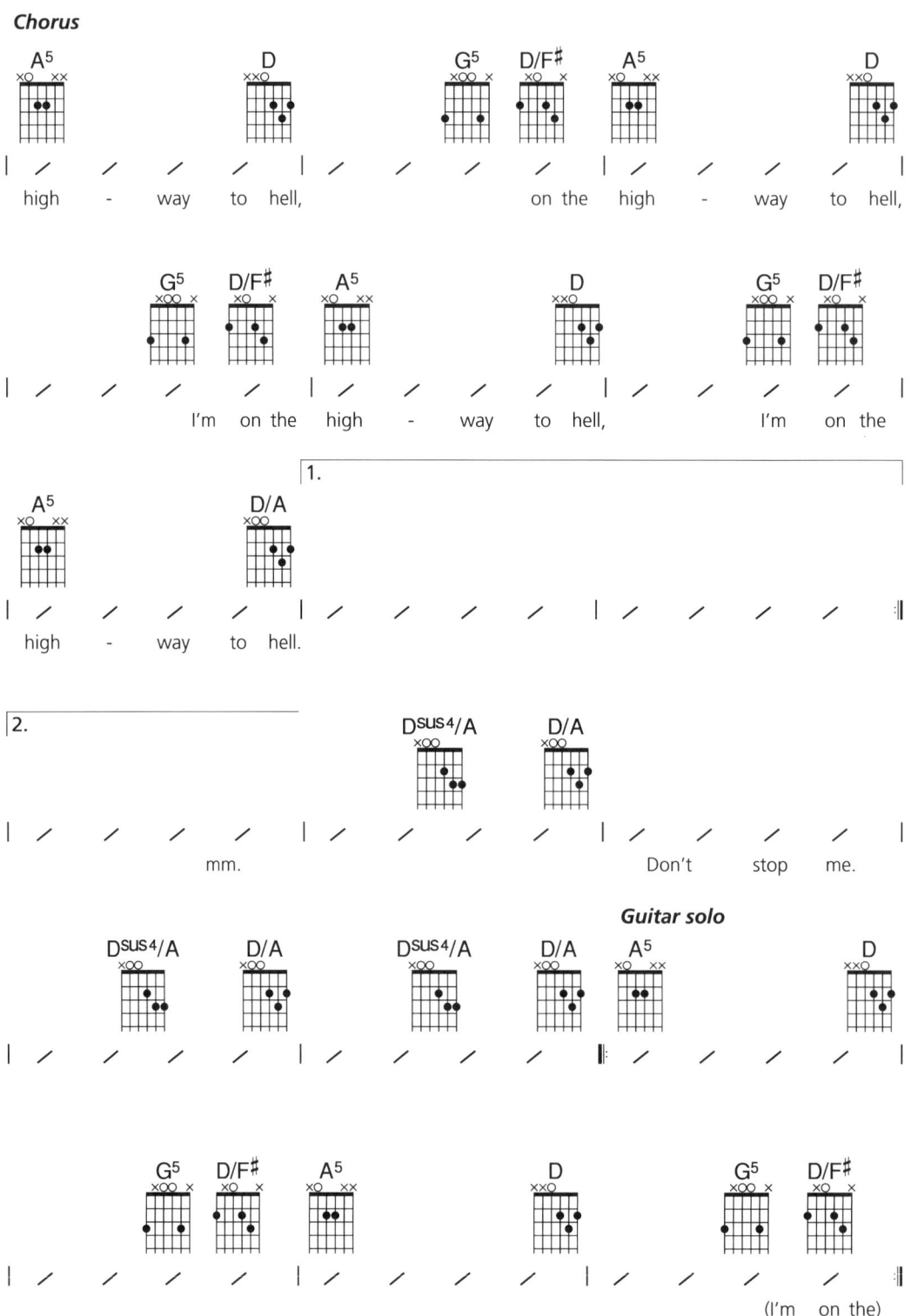

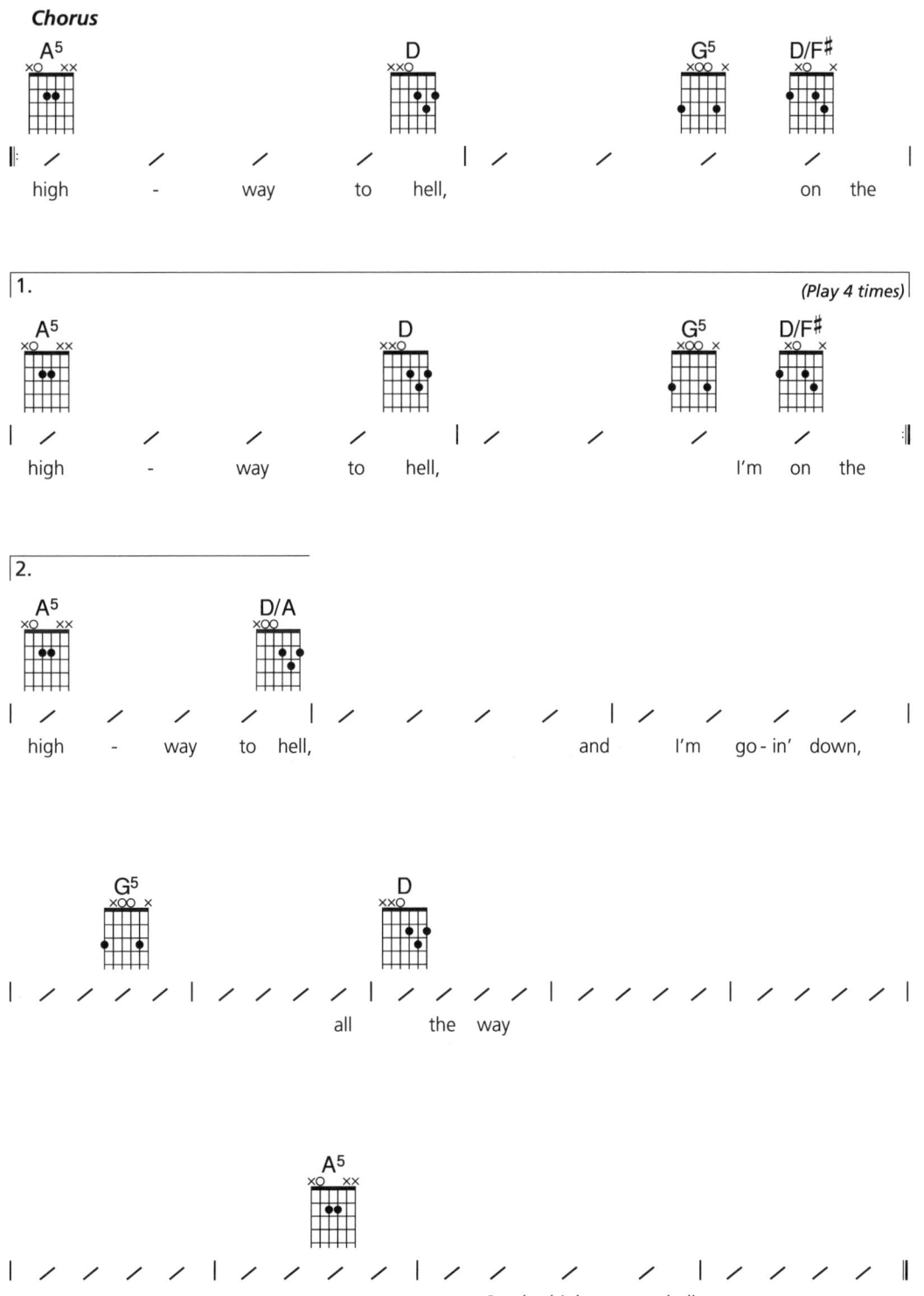

How Deep Is Your Love

Words & Music by Barry Gibb, Maurice Gibb & Robin Gibb

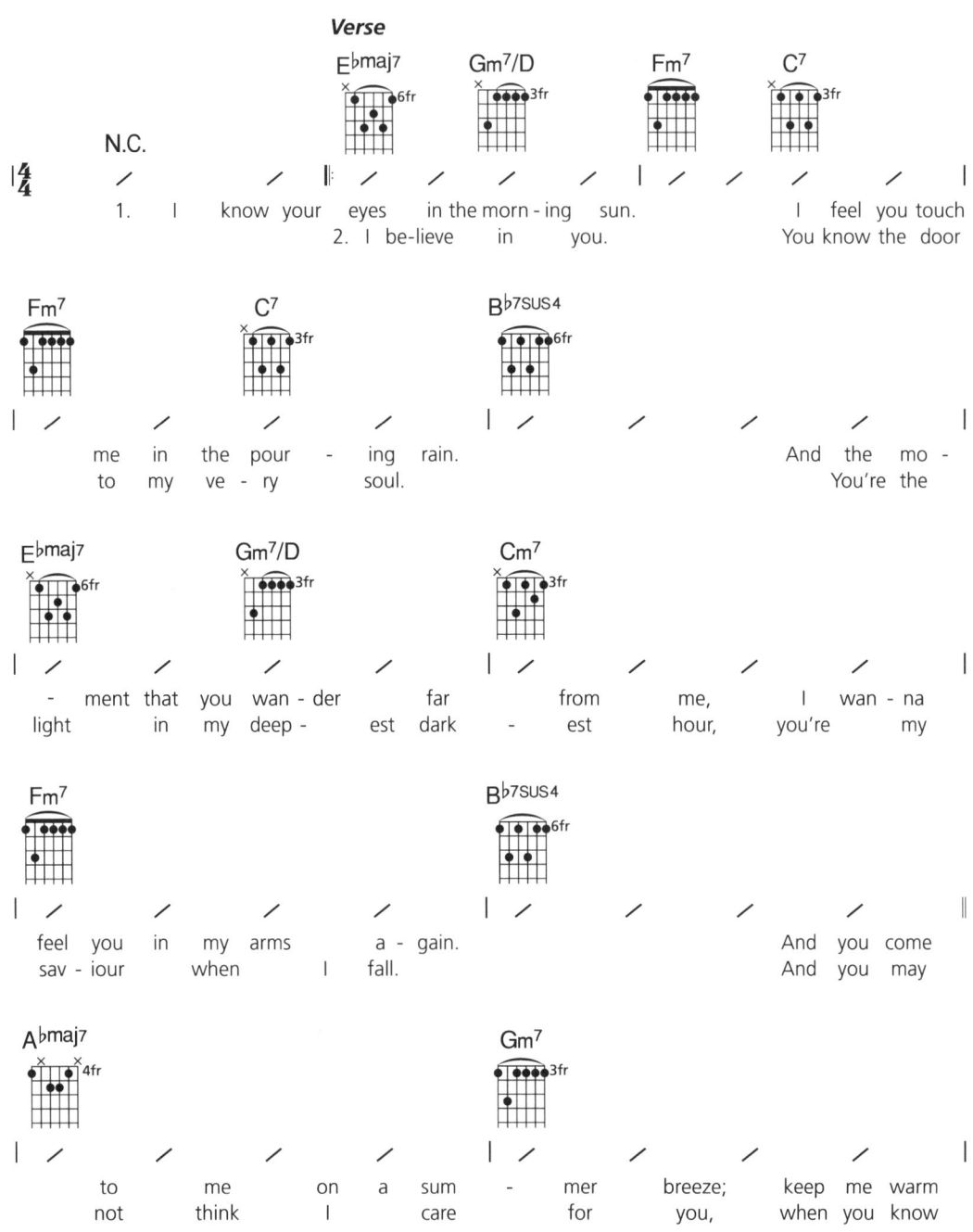

© Copyright 1977 Gibb Brothers Music/Universal Music Publishing MGB Limited (66.66%)
(Administered in Germany by Musik Edition Discoton GmbH., A Division of Universal Music Publishing Group)/
Crompton Songs/Warner/Chappell Music Limited (33.34%).
All Rights Reserved. International Copyright Secured.

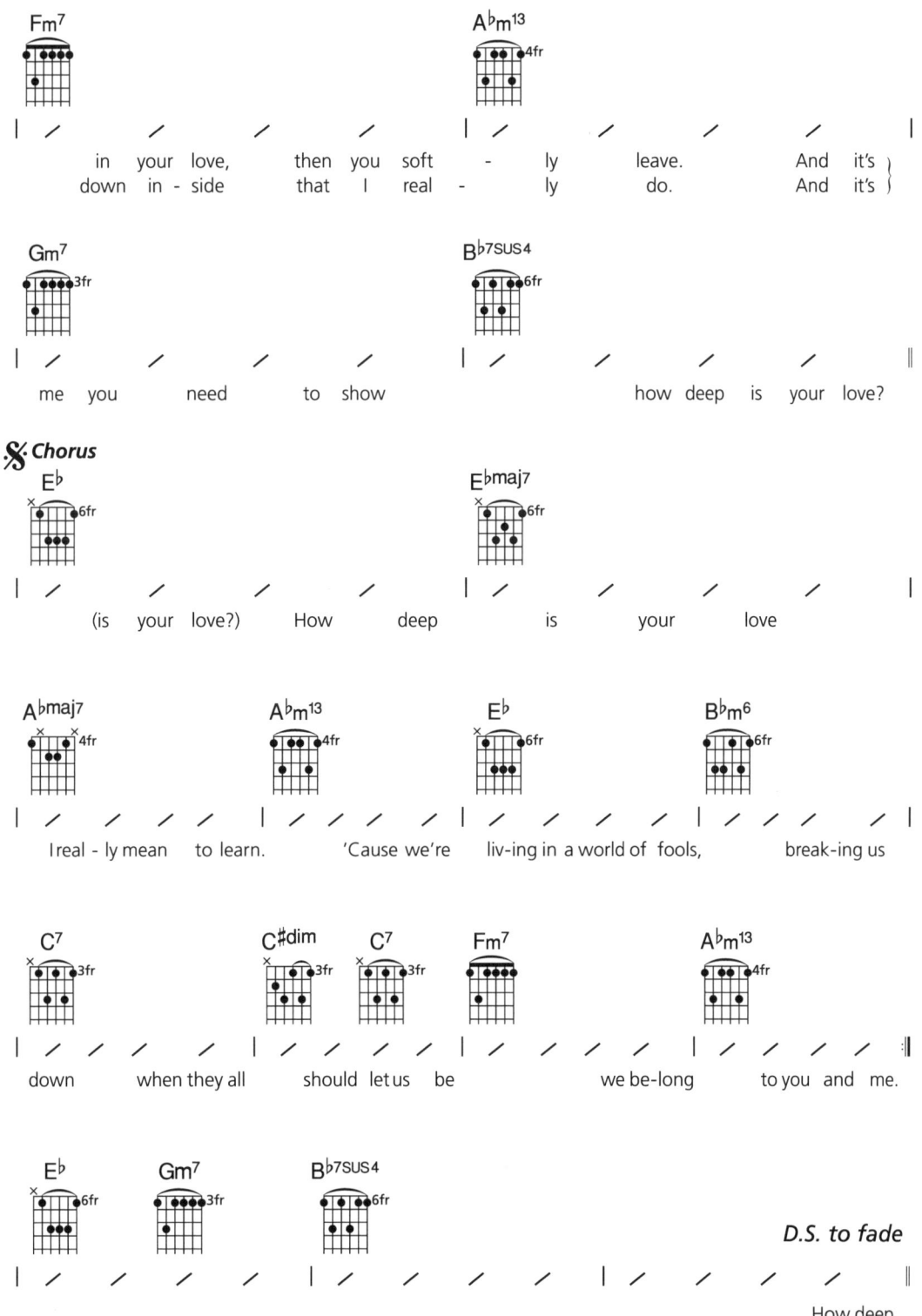

I Predict A Riot

Words & Music by Nicholas Hodgson, Richard Wilson, Andrew White, James Rix & Nicholas Baines

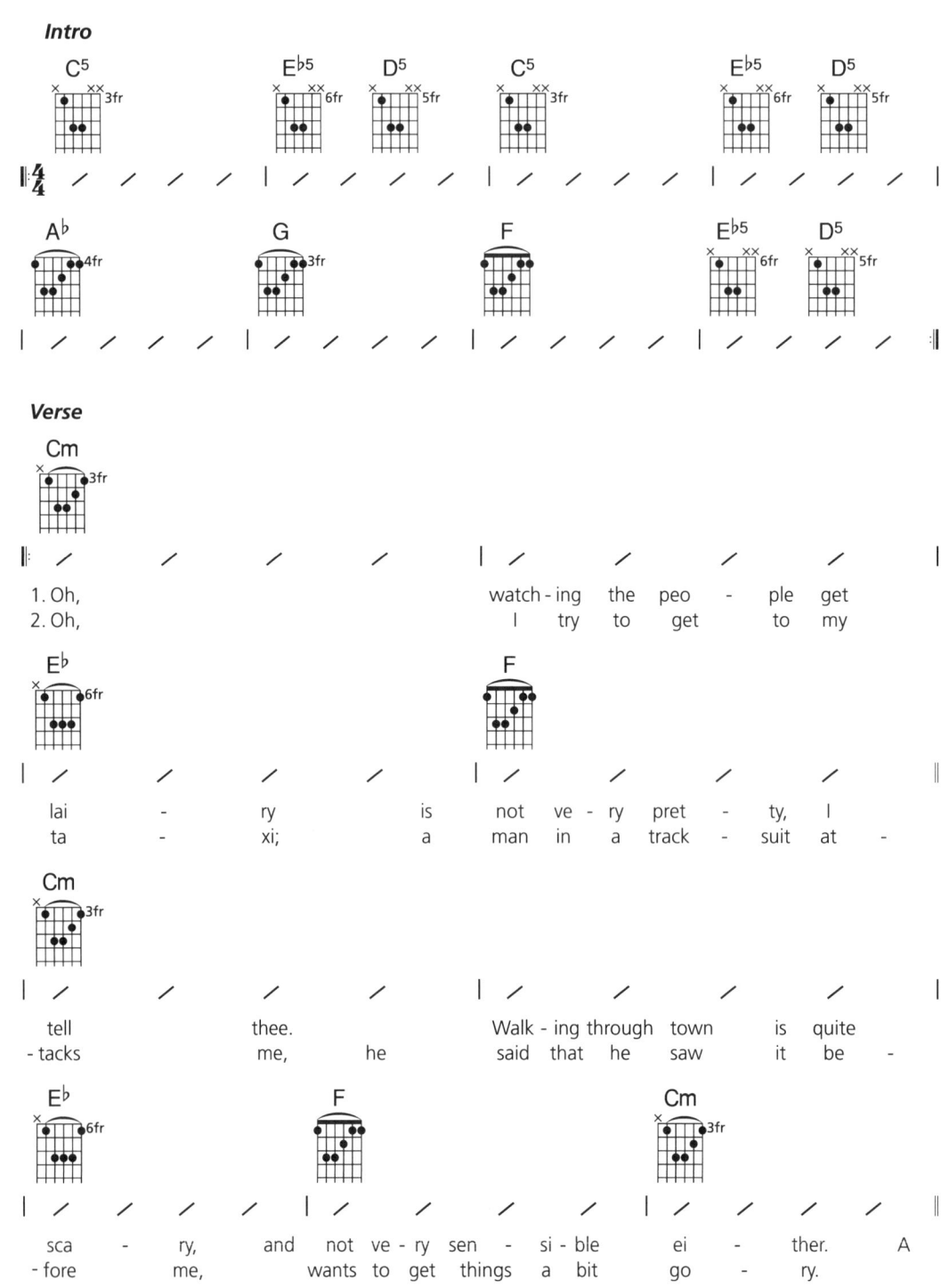

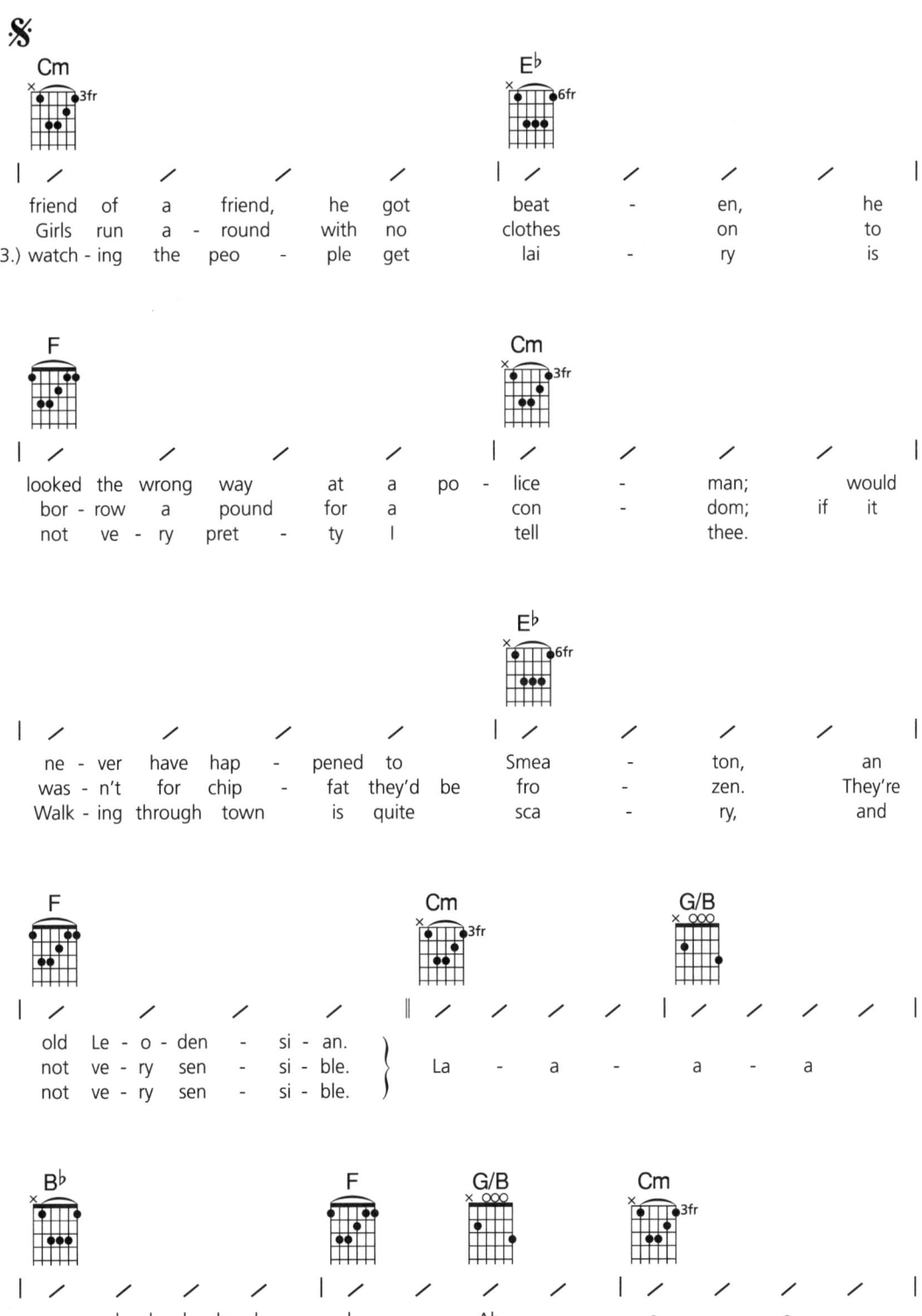

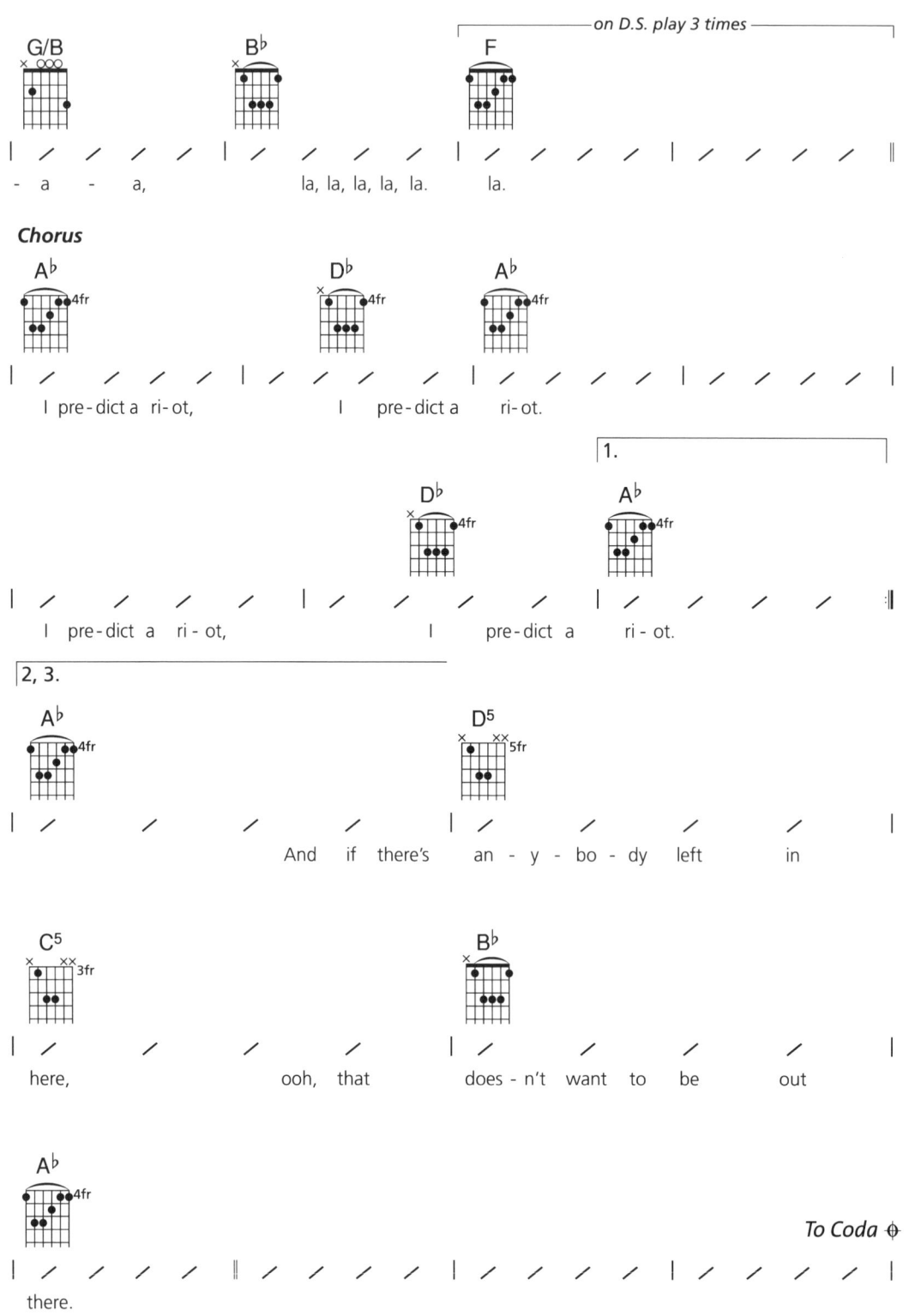

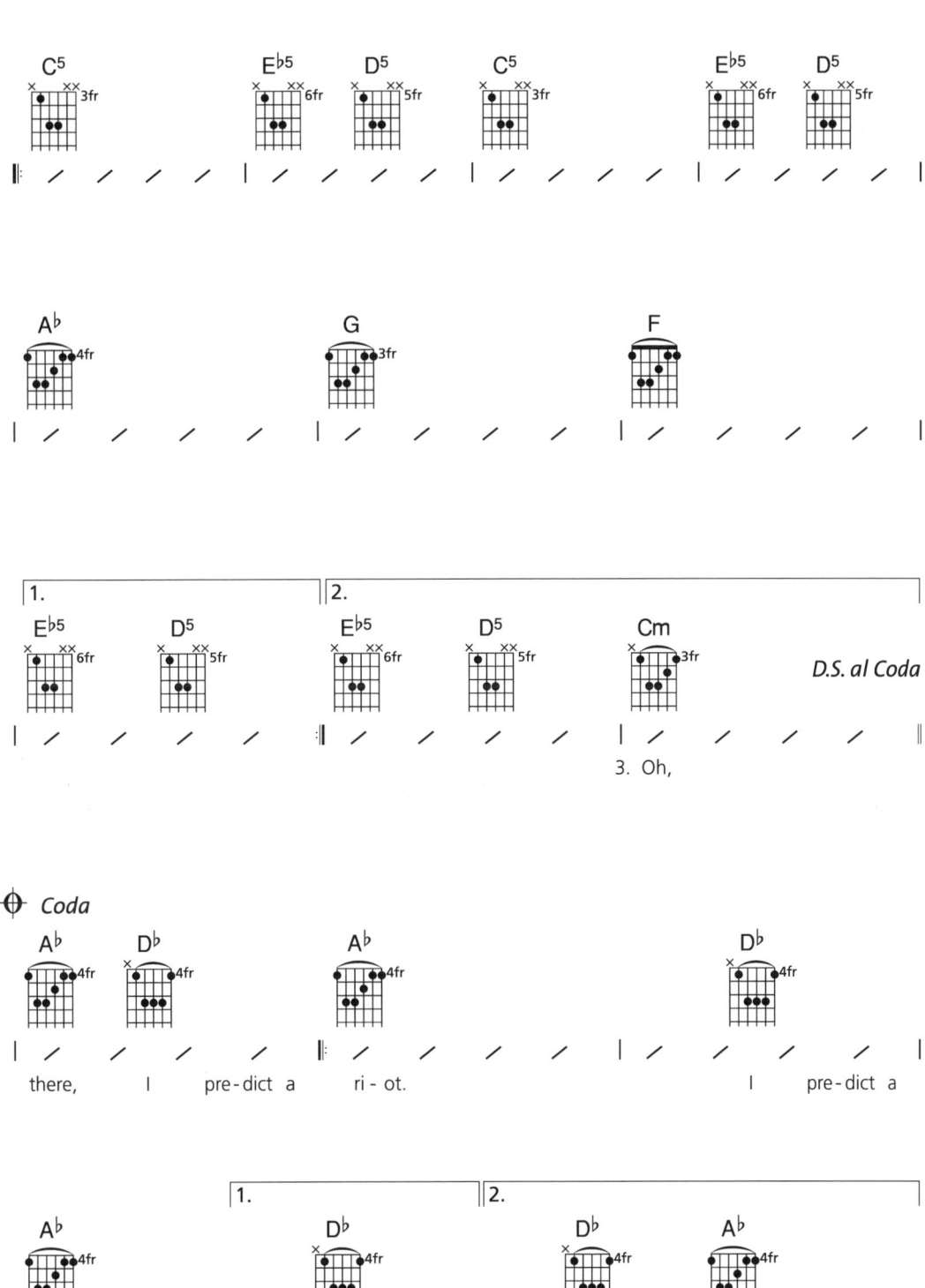

I Shot The Sheriff

Words & Music by Bob Marley

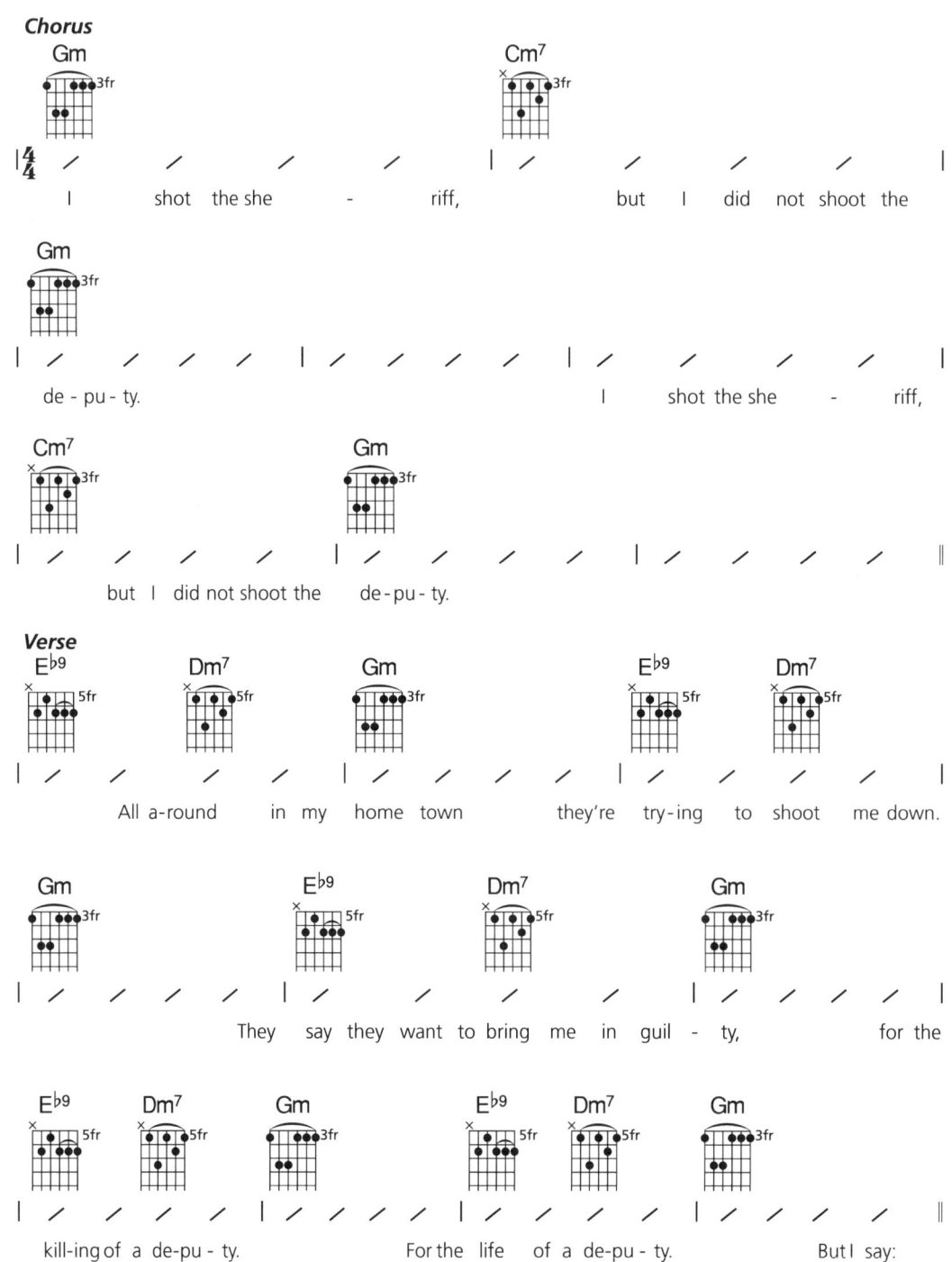

© Copyright 1973 Fifty-Six Hope Road Music Limited/Odnil Music Limited.
Blue Mountain Music Limited.
All Rights Reserved. International Copyright Secured.

Riff

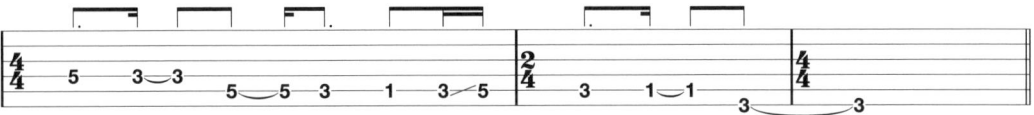

Chorus 2
I shot the sheriff
But I swear it was in self defence.
I shot the sheriff
And they say it is a capital offence.

Verse 2
Sheriff John Brown always hated me
For what I don't know
And every time that I plant a seed
He said "Kill it, before it grows."
He said "Kill it, before it grows."

Chorus 3
I shot the sheriff
But I swear it was in self defence
I shot the sheriff
And they say it is a capital offence.

Verse 3
Freedom came my way one day
And I started out of town there.
All of a sudden I see Sheriff John Brown
Aiming to shot me down
So I shot, I shot him down,
And I say

Chorus 4 & 5
I shot the sheriff
But I did not shoot the deputy.
I shot the sheriff
But I did not shoot the deputy.

Verse 4
Reflexes got the better of me
And what must be must be.
Every day the bucket goes to the well
But one day the bottom will drop out,
Yes, one day the bottom will drop out.

I Will Survive

Words & Music by Dino Fekaris & Freddie Perren

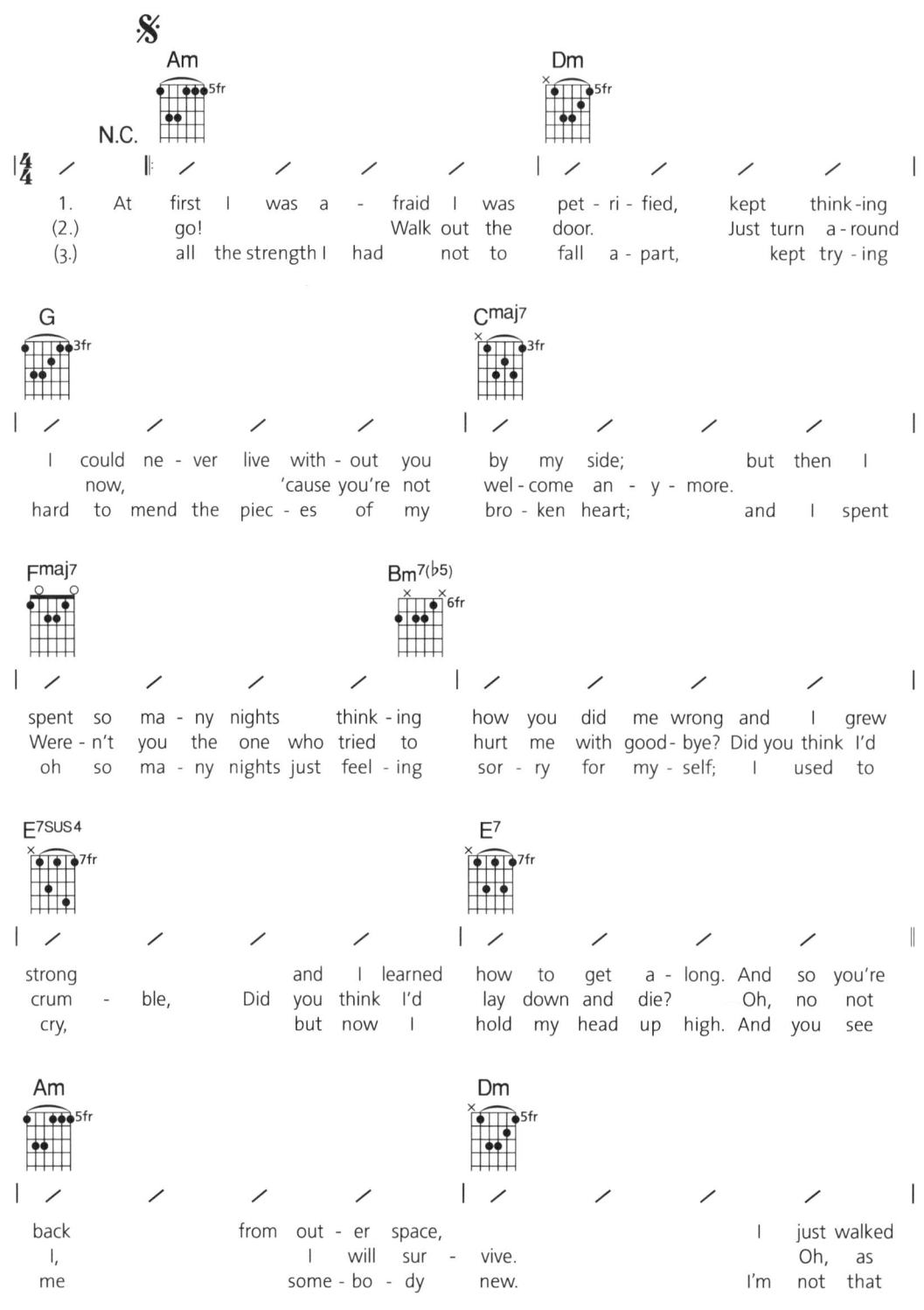

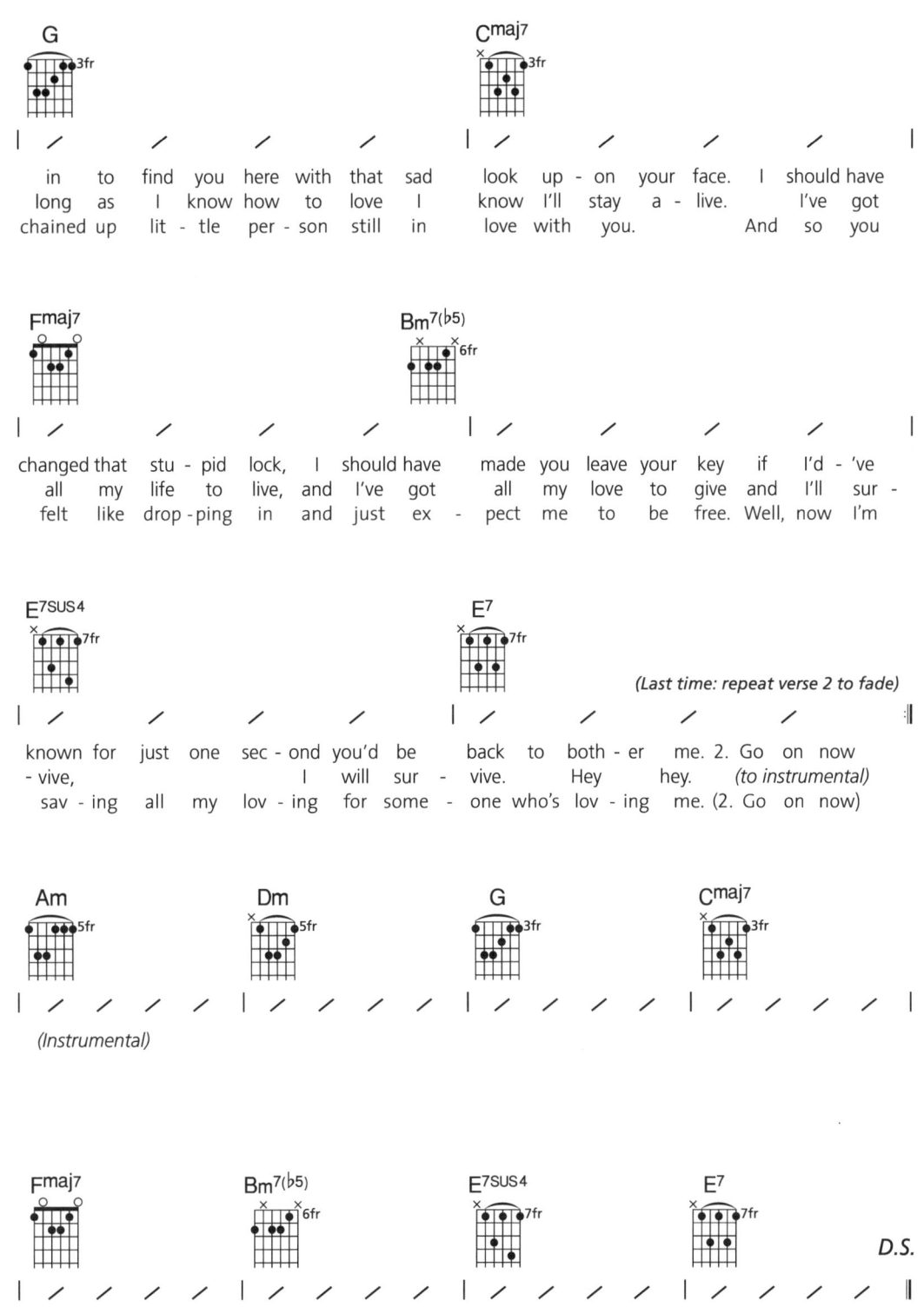

Is You Is Or Is You Ain't My Baby?
(from 'Five Guys Named Moe')

Words & Music by Billy Austin & Louis Jordan

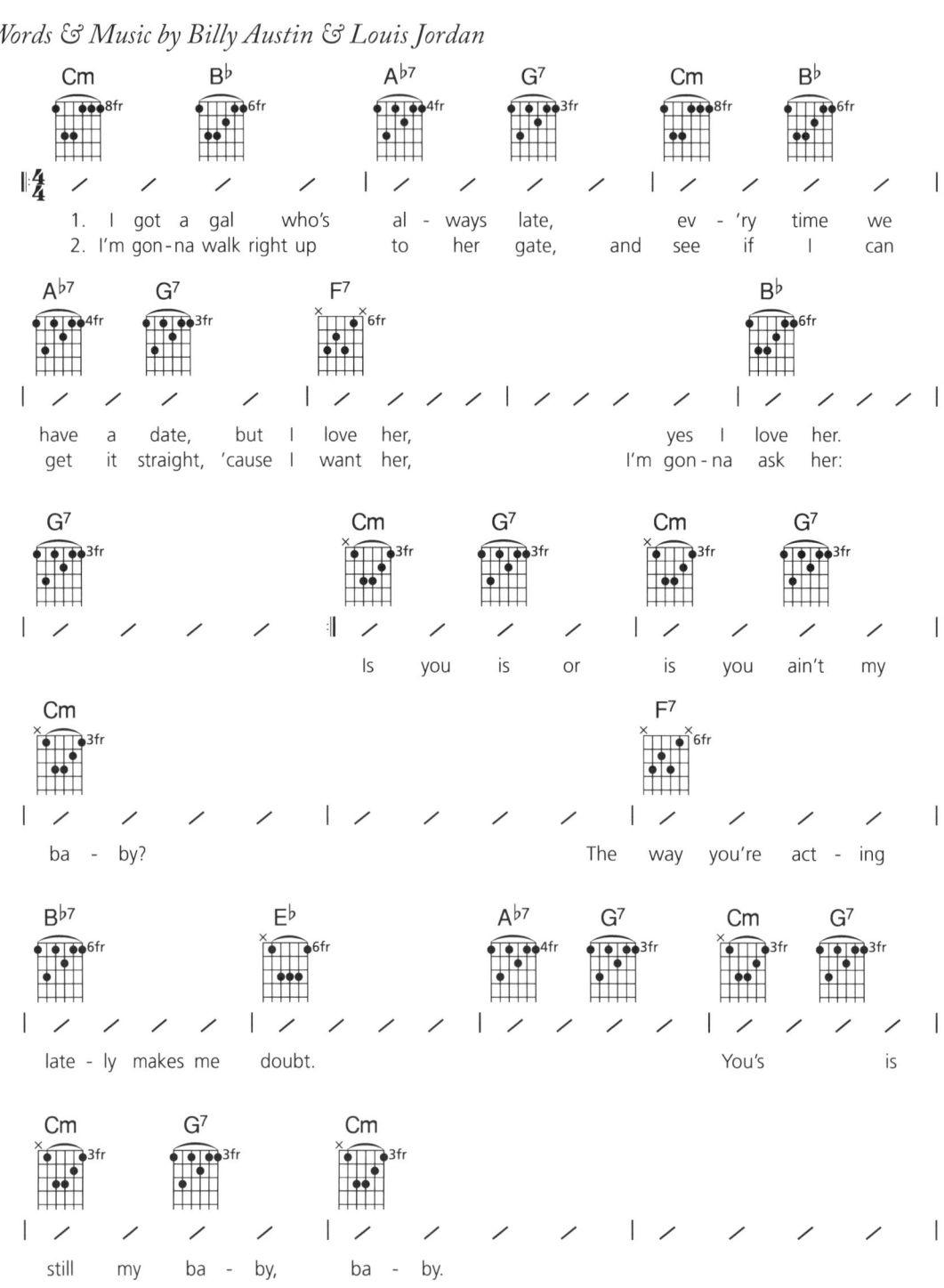

© Copyright 1943 & 1944 Leeds Music Corporation, USA.
Universal/MCA Music Limited.
All rights in Germany administered by Universal/MCA Music Publ. GmbH.
All Rights Reserved. International Copyright Secured.

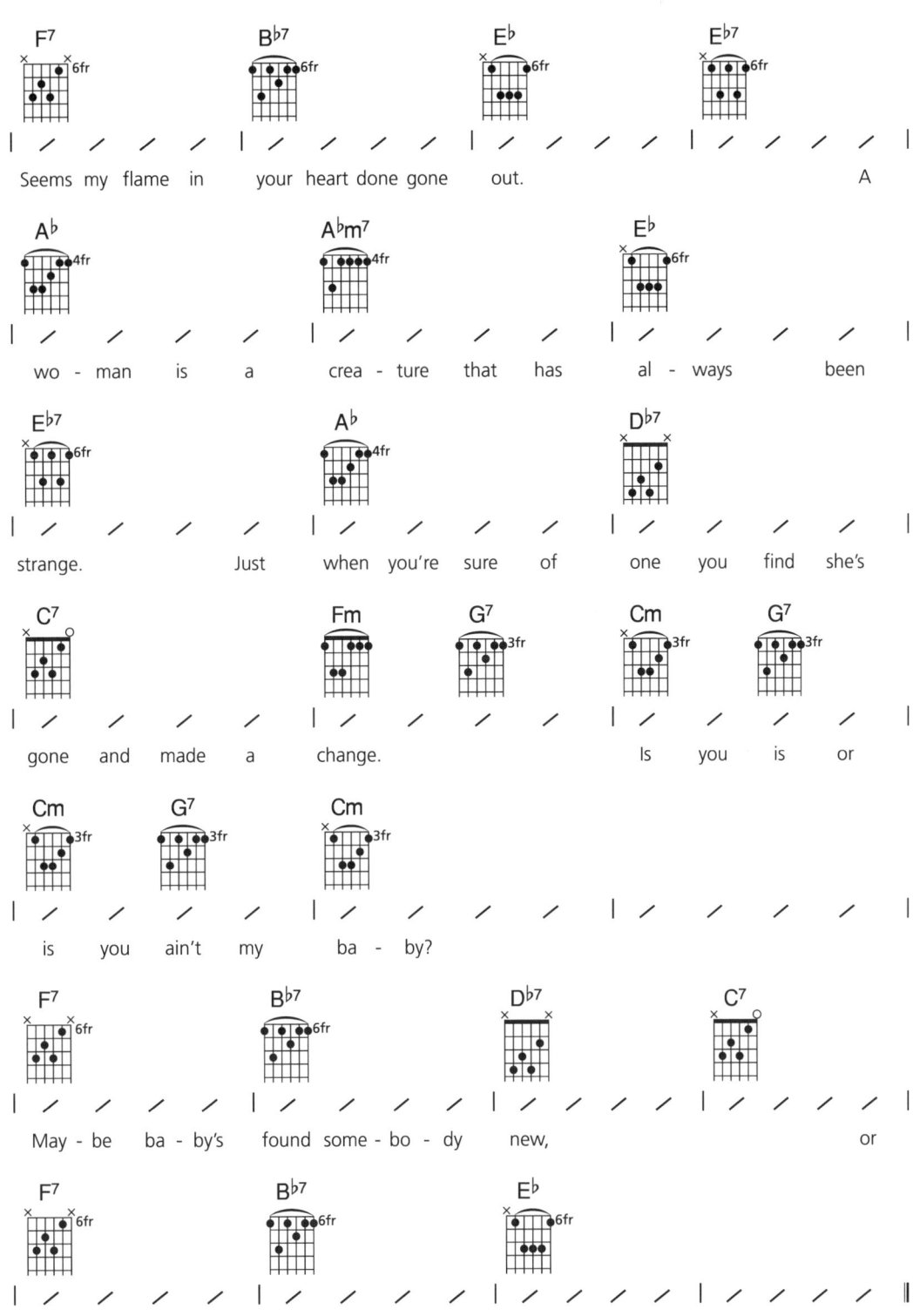

Run

Words & Music by Gary Lightbody, Jonathan Quinn, Mark McClelland, Nathan Connolly & Iain Archer

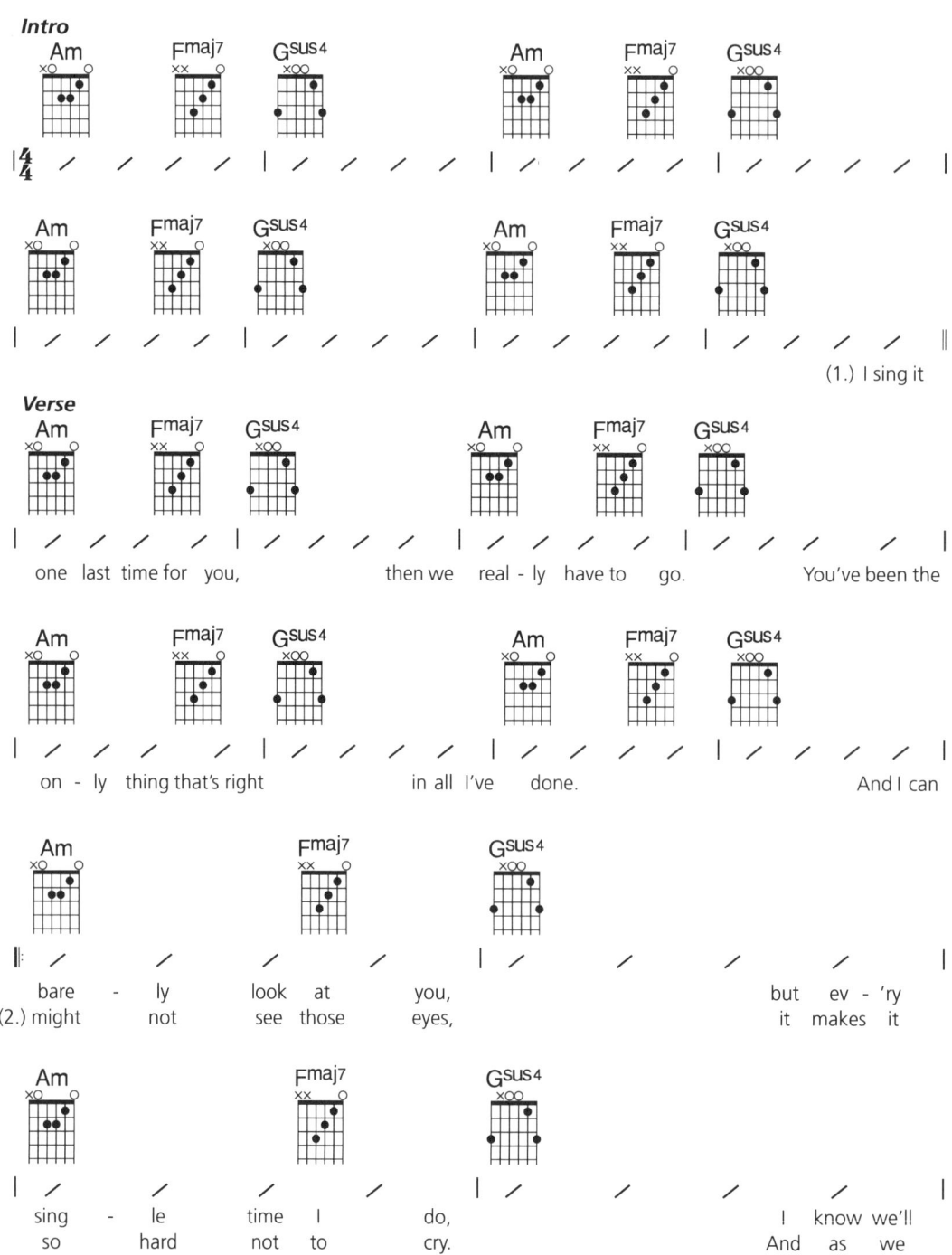

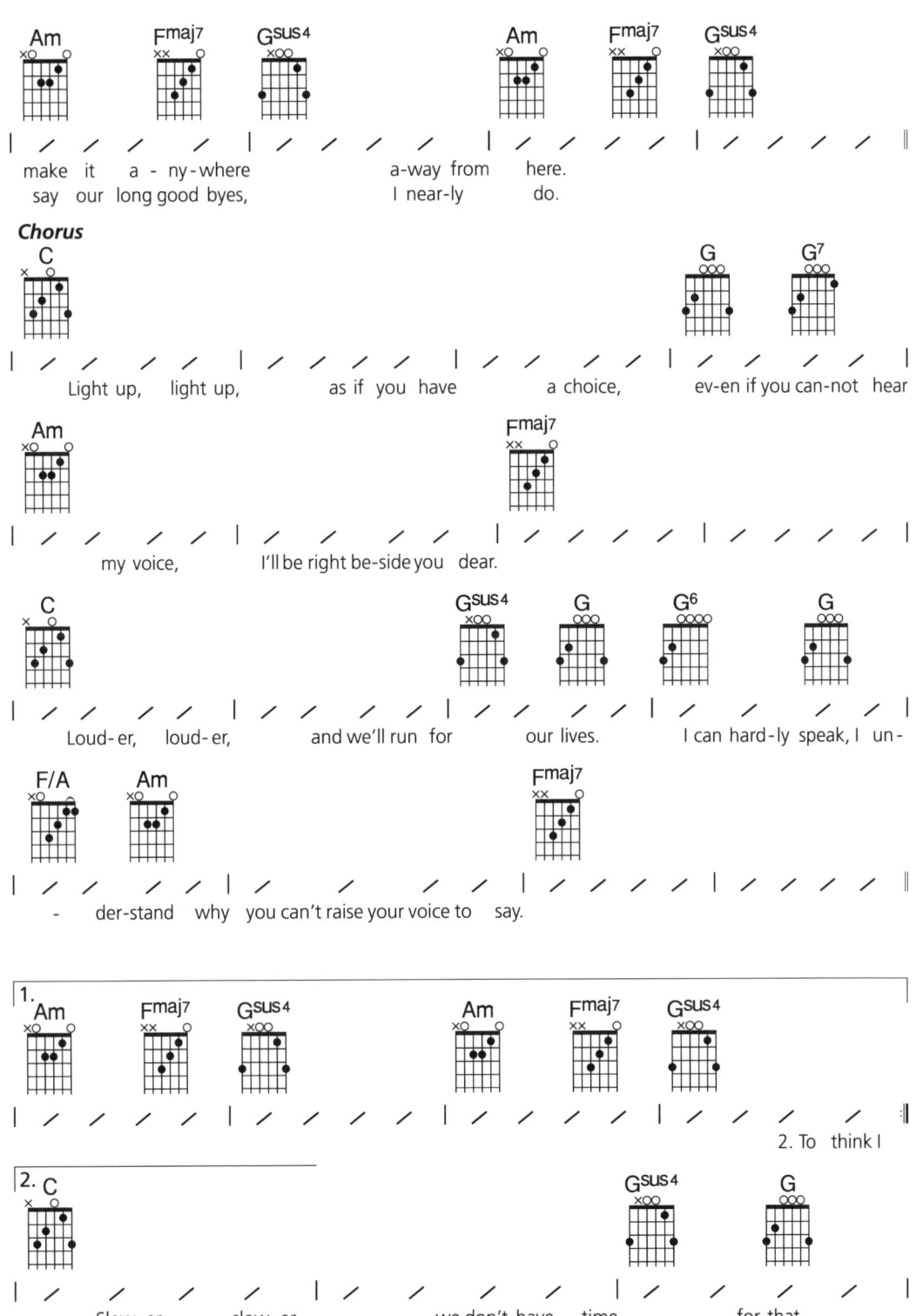

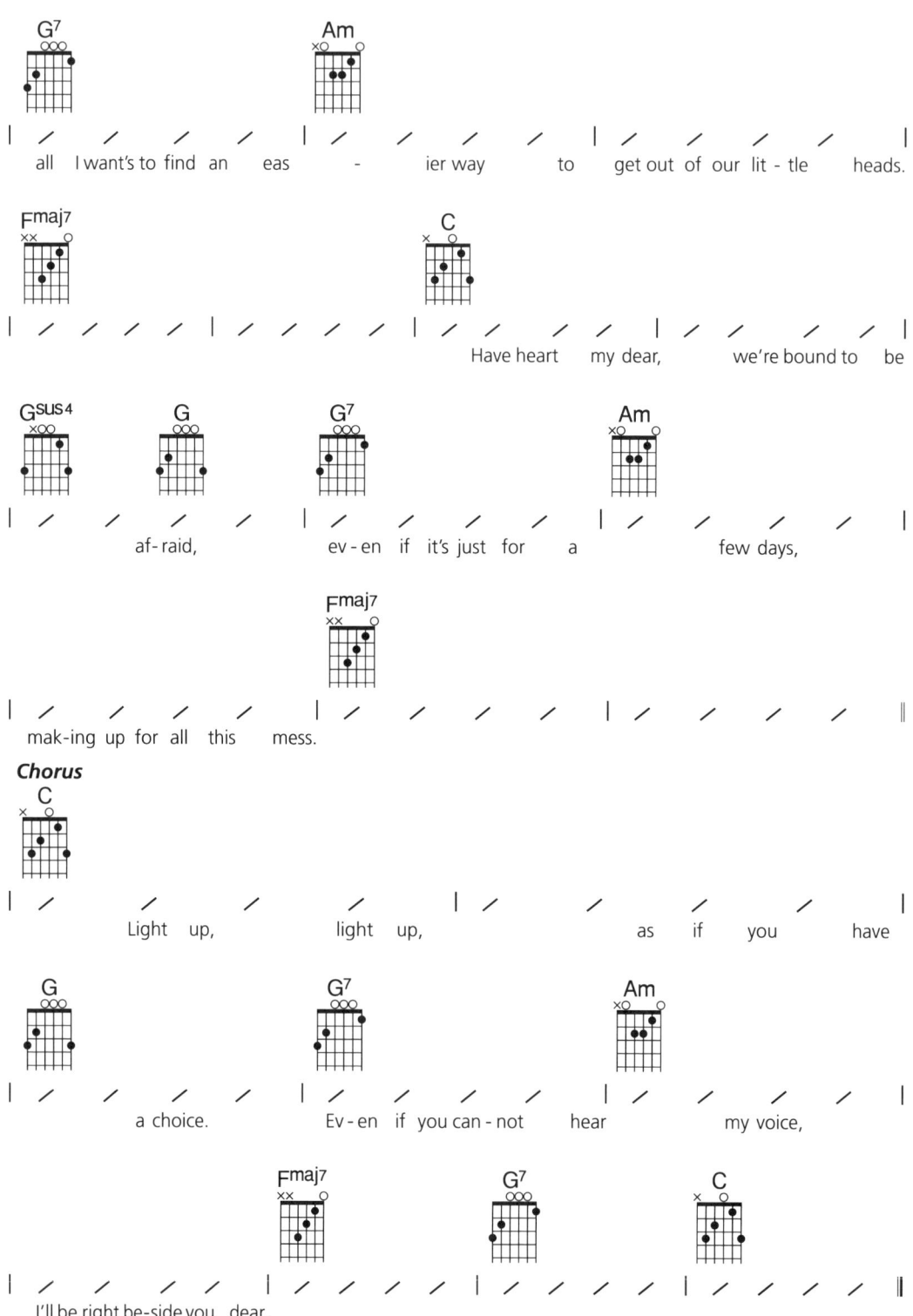

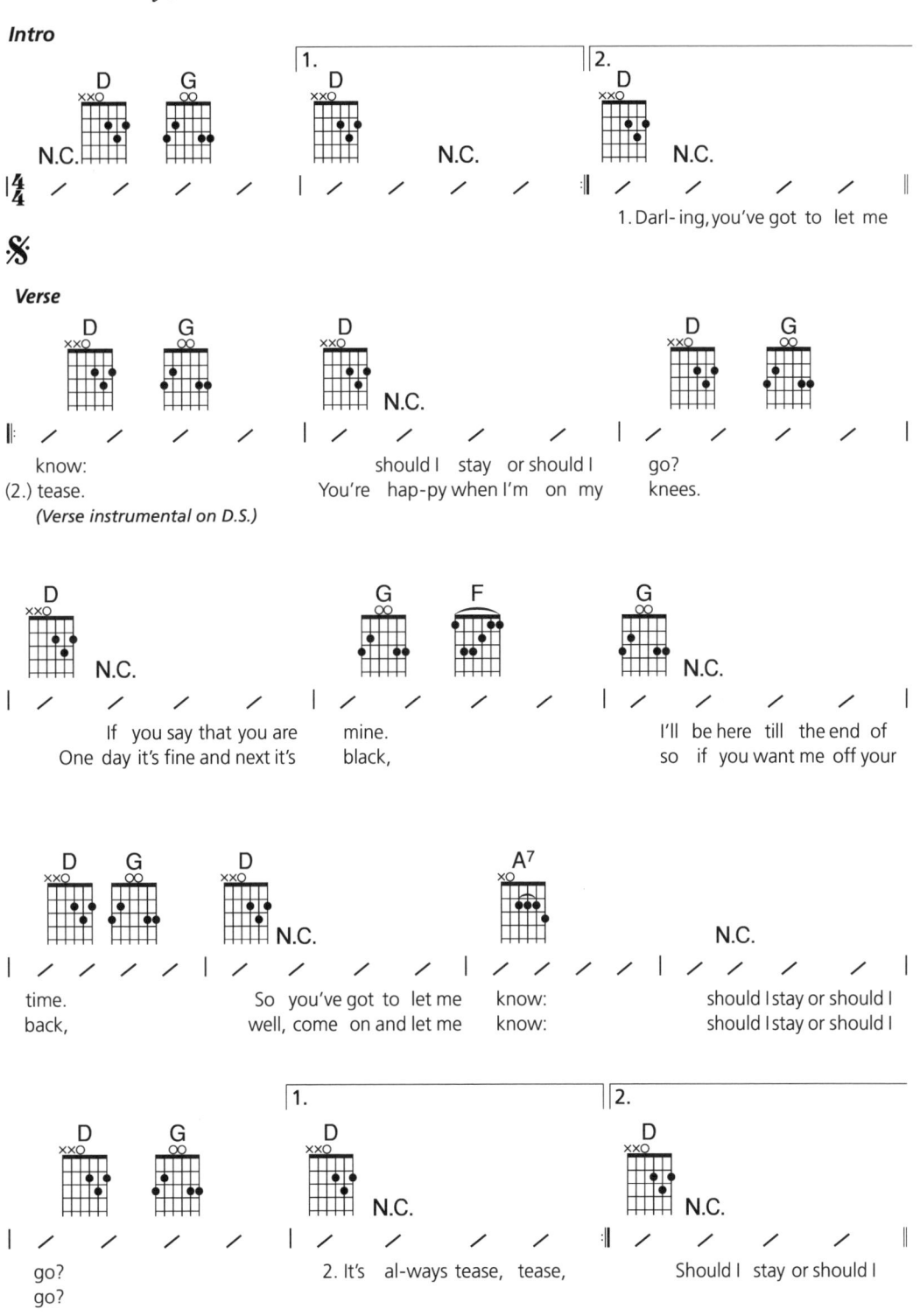

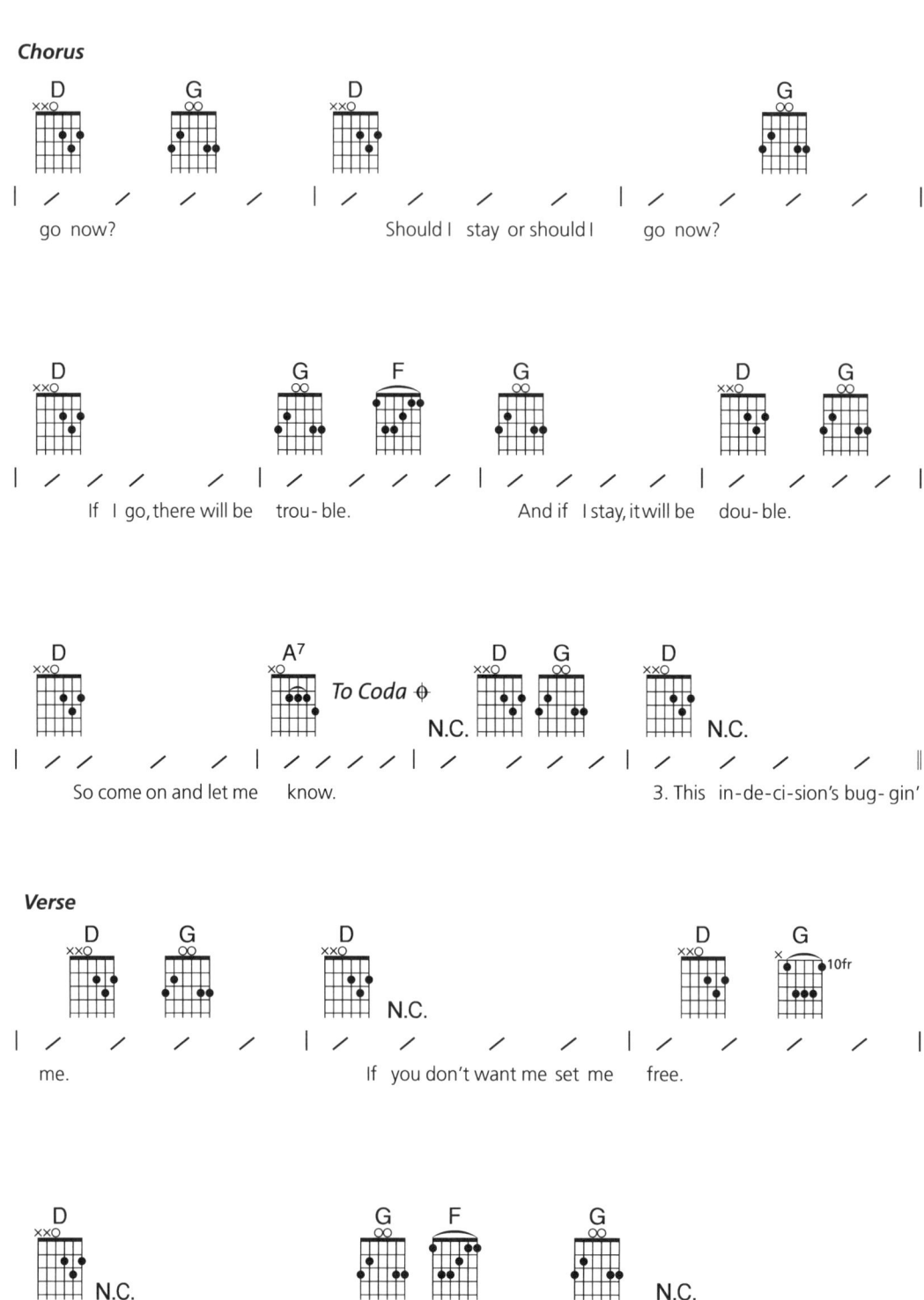

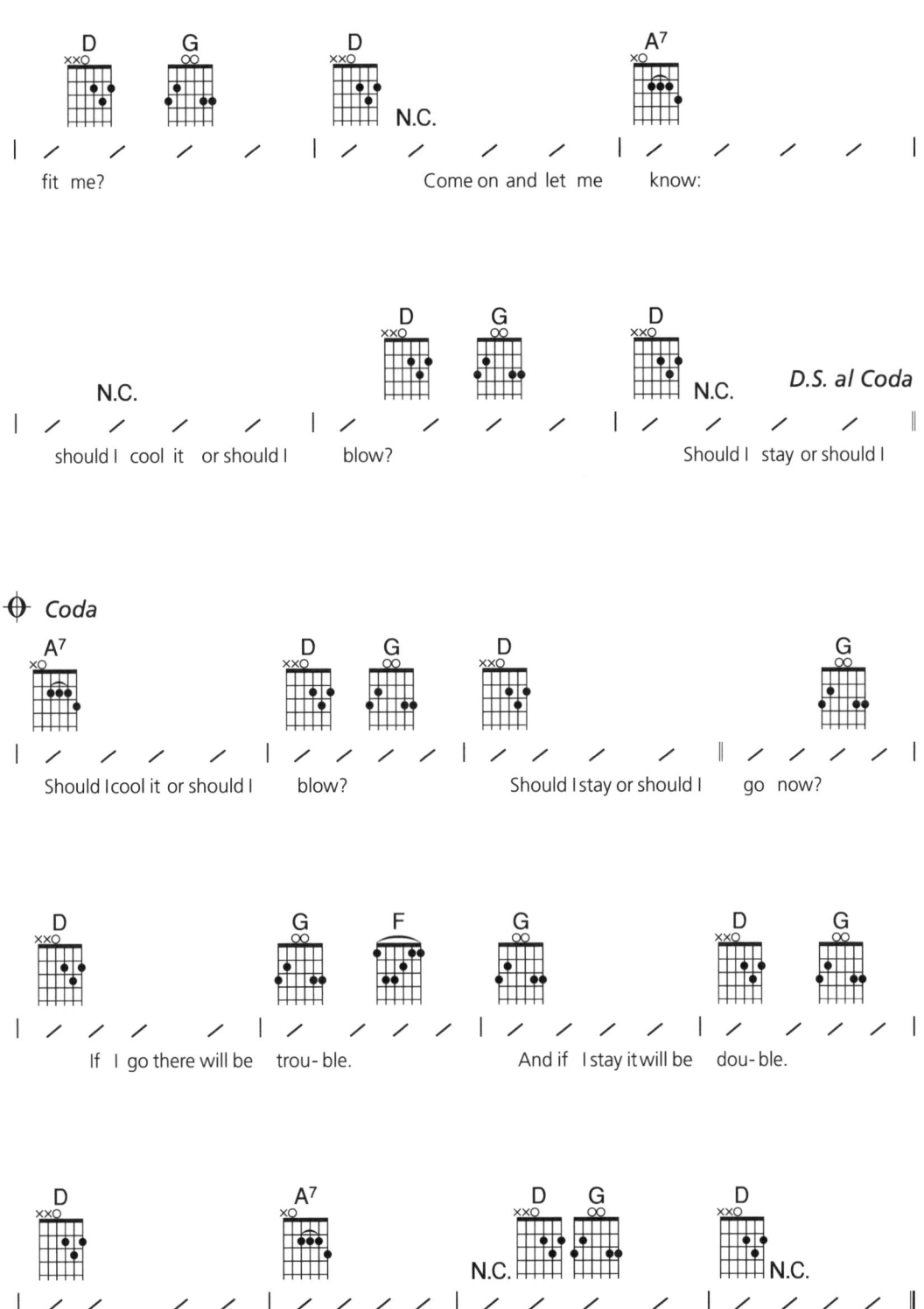

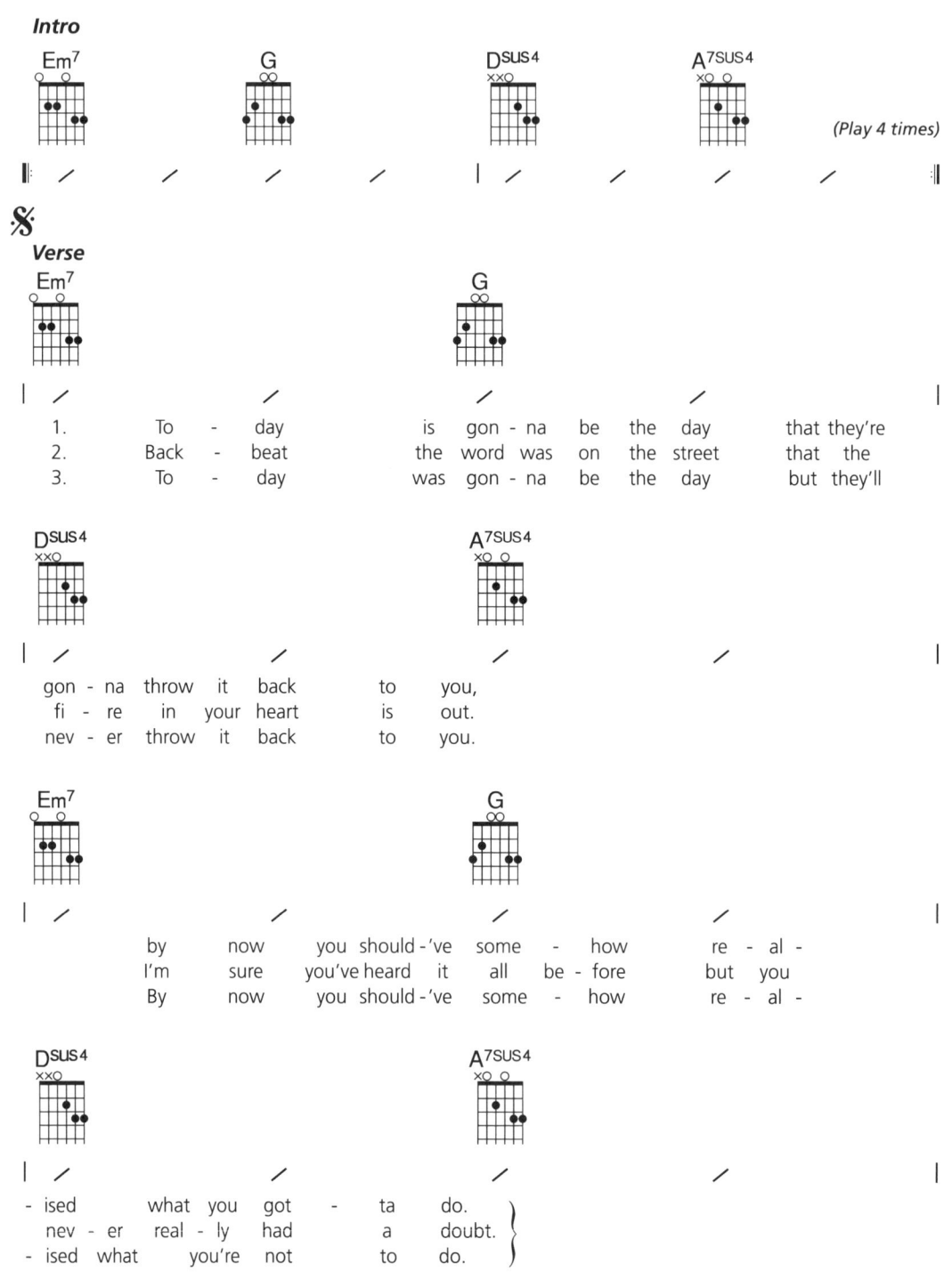

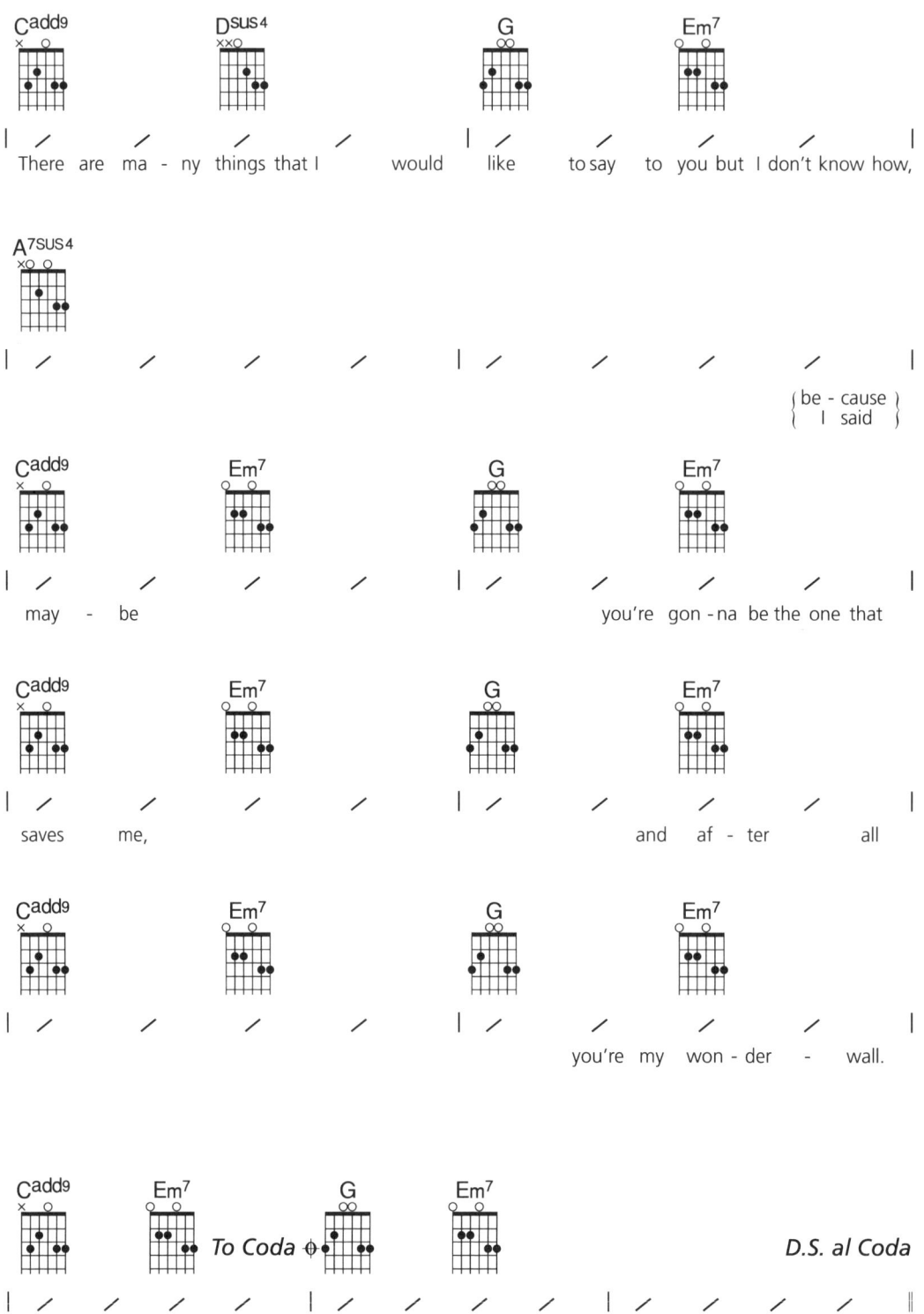

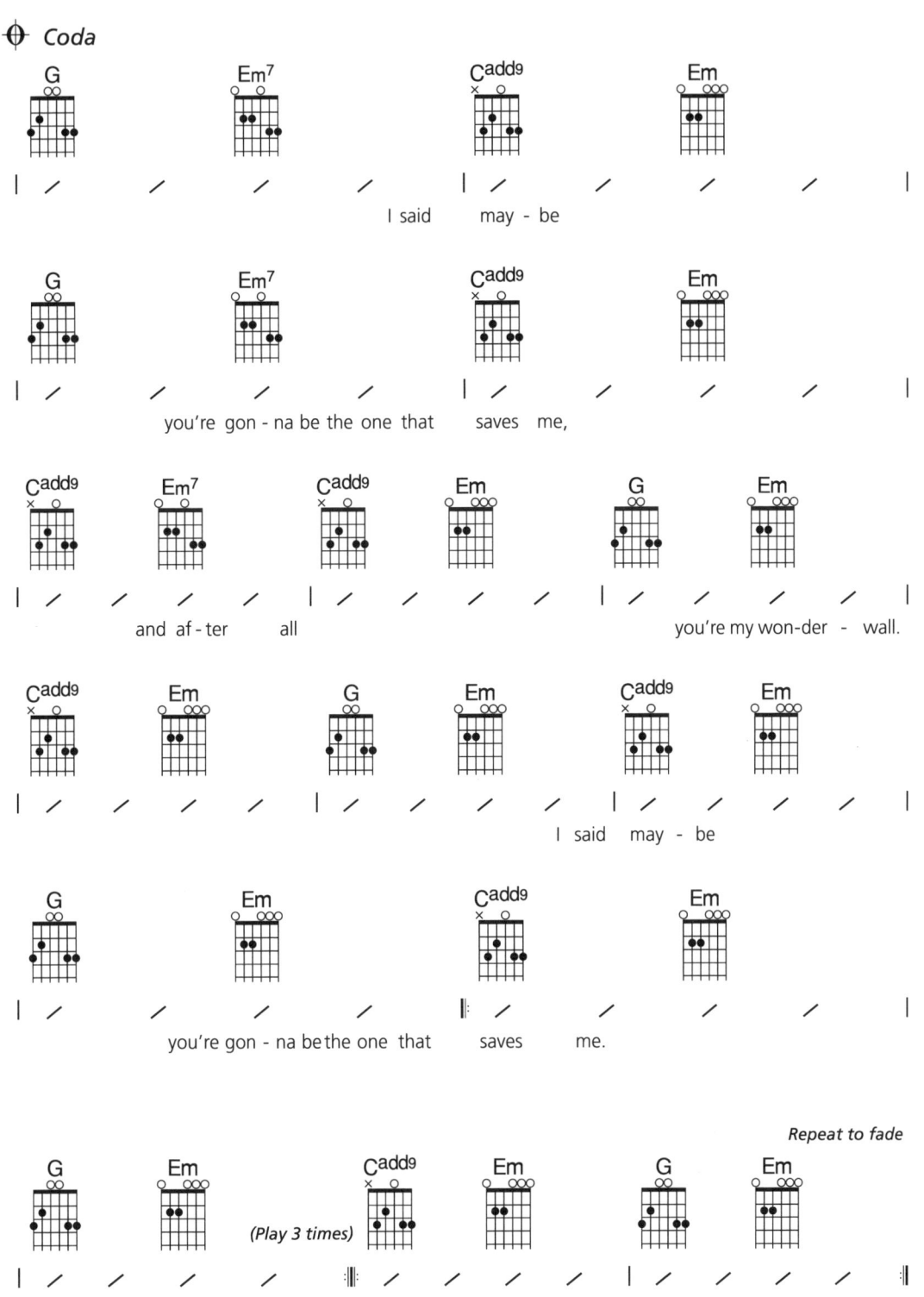

Viva La Vida

Words & Music by Guy Berryman, Jon Buckland, Will Champion & Chris Martin

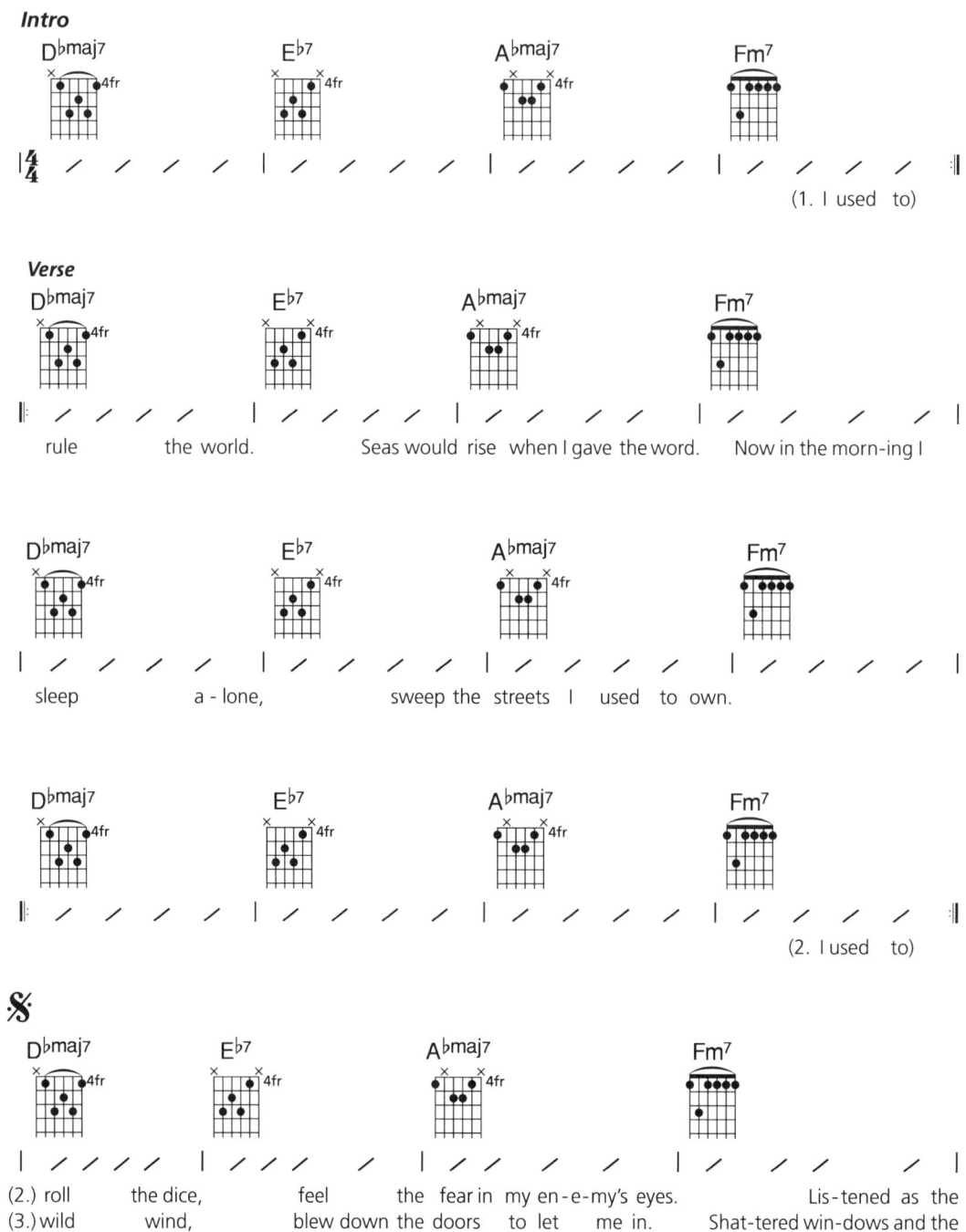

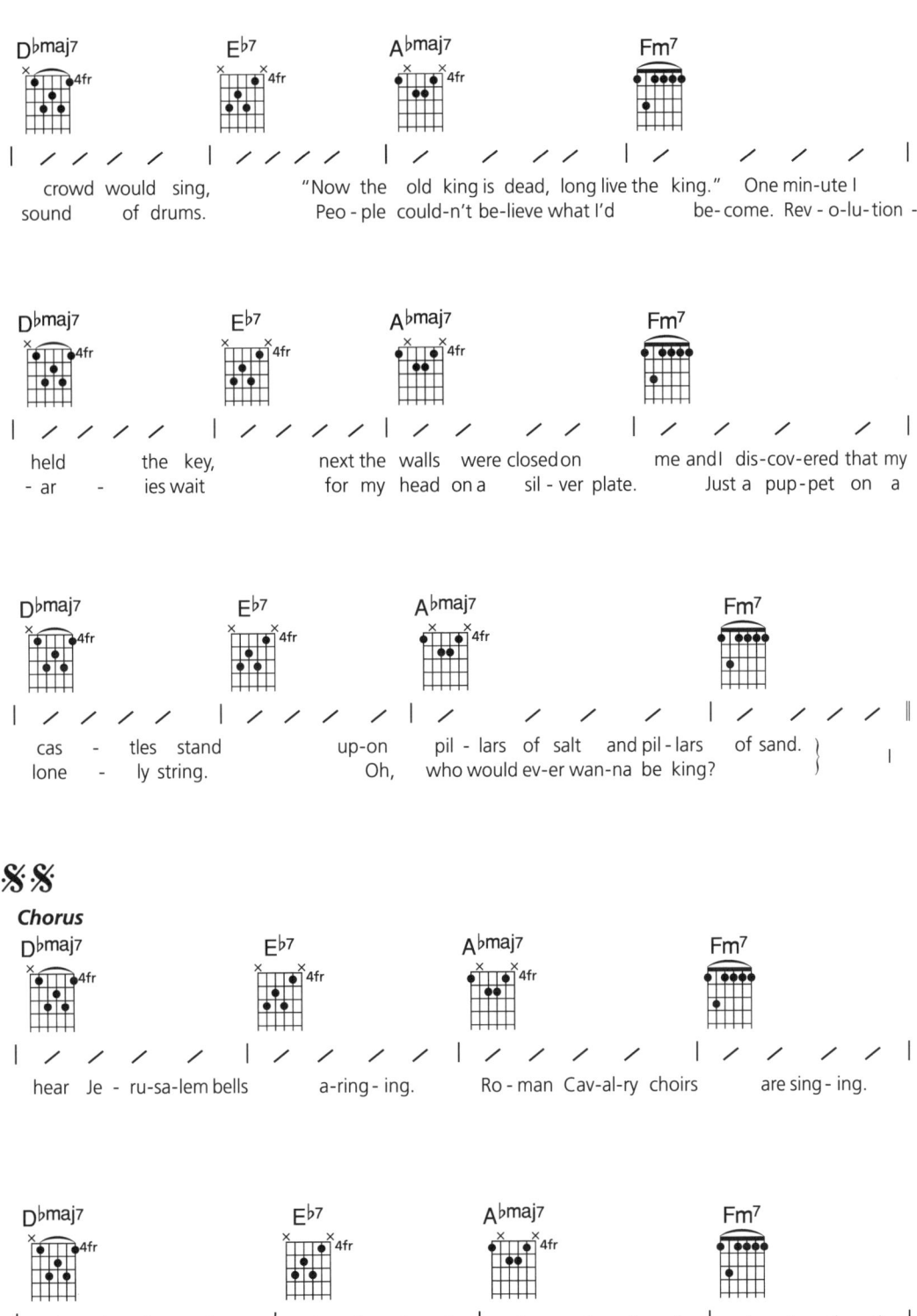

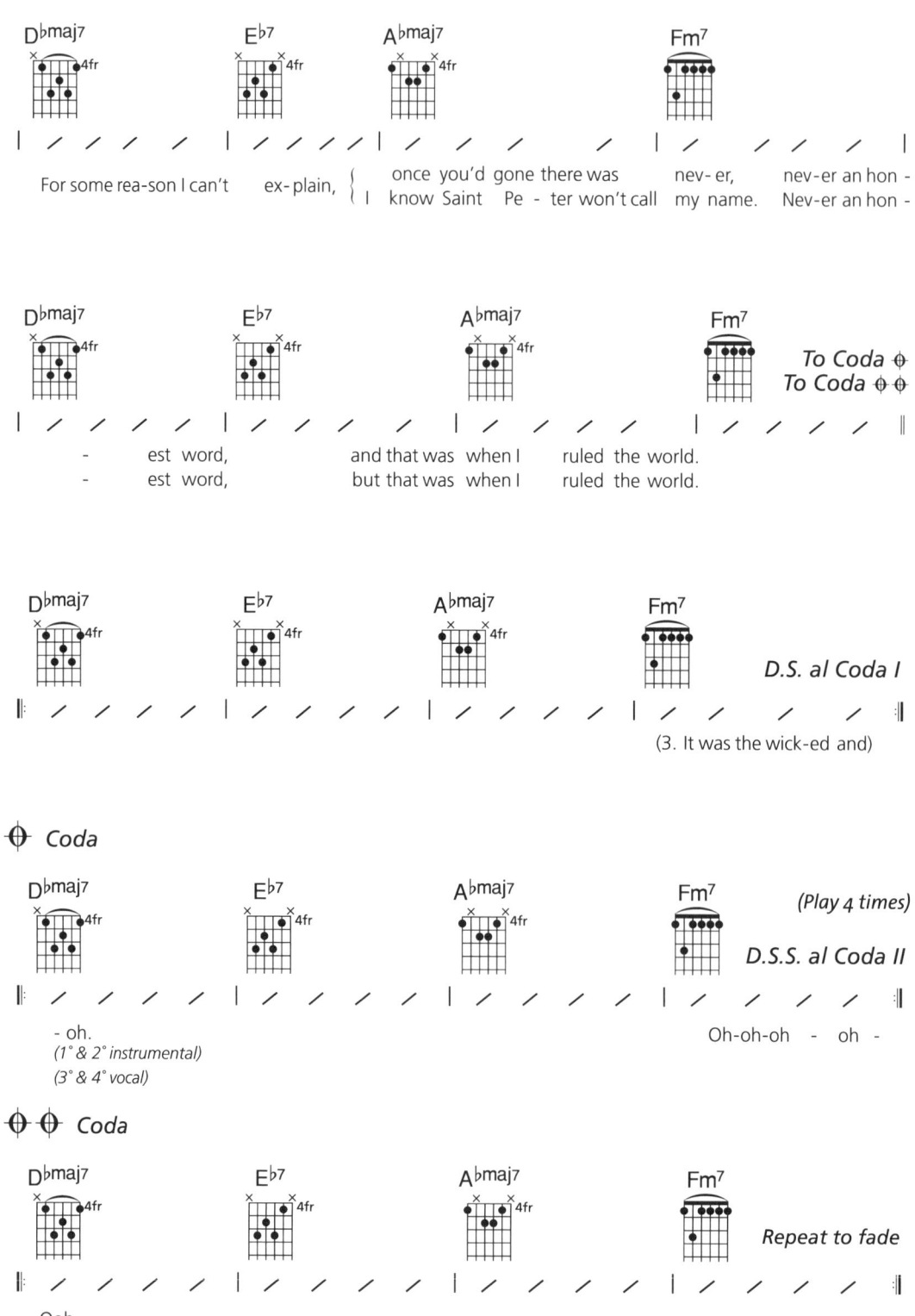

You Raise Me Up

Words & Music by Brendan Graham & Rolf Løvland

(To match original recording, use a capo 1st fret)

4/4 N.C. / / / / ‖: **D** / / / **Dsus4** / / / **D** / / |
When I am down, and oh my soul so weary, when trou-bles

| **D** / / / **G** / / / | **A** / / / **G** / / |
come and my heart bur-dened be, then I am still, and wait here in the

| **D** / / / **G** / / / | **D** / / / **A** / / / | **D** / / / / / / ‖
si - lence, un - til you come and sit a while with me. You raise me

| **Bm** / / / **G** / / / | **D** / / / **A** / / / | **Bm** / / / **G** / / / |
up so I can stand on moun - tains. You raise me up to walk on storm-y

| **D** / / / **A** / / / | **D** / / / **G** / / / |
seas. I am strong when I am on your

| **D** / / / **G** / / / | **D** / / / **Asus4** / **A** / | **D** / / / N.C. / / / |
shoul - ders. You raise me up to more than I can be. You raise me

© Copyright 2001 Universal Music AS, Norway/Peermusic (Ireland) Limited
Universal-Polygram International Publishing, Inc./Alfred Publishing Company, Inc. (50%)/
Peermusic (UK) Limited (50%).
All Rights Reserved. International Copyright Secured.

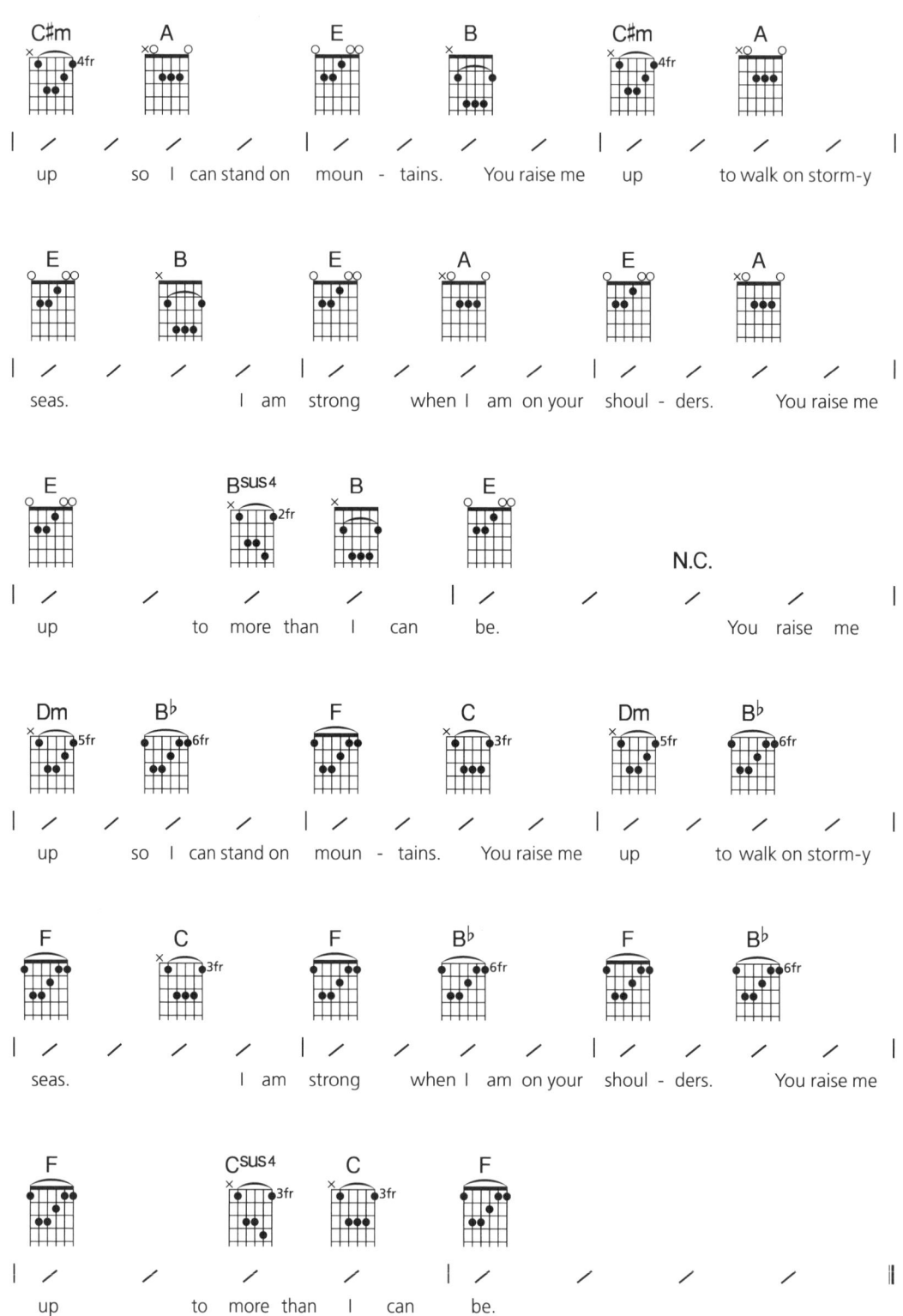